Physical Characteristics of the German Shepherd Dog

(from the American Kennel Club breed standard)

Withers: Higher than and sloping into the level back.

Back: Straight, very strongly developed without sag or roach, and relatively short.

Hindquarters: The whole assembly of the thigh, viewed from the side, is broad, with both upper and lower thigh well muscled, forming as nearly as possible a right angle. The upper thigh bone parallels the shoulder blade while the lower thigh bone parallels the upper arm. The metatarsus (the unit between the hock joint and the foot) is short, strong and tightly articulated.

Ribs: Well sprung and long, neither barrel-shaped nor too flat, and carried down to a sternum which reaches to the elbows.

Abdomen: Firmly held and not paunchy. The bottom line is only moderately tucked up in the loin.

Tail: Bushy, with the last vertebra extended at least to the hock joint. It is set smoothly into the croup and low rather than high. At rest, the tail hangs in a slight curve like a saber.

Coat: A double coat of medium length. The outer coat should be as dense as possible, hair straight, harsh and lying close to the body.

Color: Various, and most colors are permissible. Strong rich colors are preferred.

Size: Males, 24 to 26 inches; and for bitches, 22 to 24 inches.

German Shepherd Dog

By Susan Samms

Contents

Photography by Isabelle Français and Carol Ann Johnson with additional photographs by:

Norvia Behling, Carolina Biological Supply, Liza Clancy, David Dalton, Marcus Degen, Fleabusters, Rx for Fleas, Detlof Handschack, James E. Hayden, RBP, James Hayden-Yoav, Alice van Kempen, Klaar, Dwight R. Kuhn, Dr. Dennis Kunkel, Alice Pantfoeder, Antonio Philippe, Phototake, Meg Purnell-Carpenter, Jean Claude Revy, M. A. Stevenson, DVM, Nikki Sussman, Christina Urban and C. James Webb.

Guide dogs pictured are trained at The Seeing Eye®, Morristown, NJ.

Drawings by Renee Low.

KENNEL CLUB BOOKS® **GERMAN SHEPHERD DOG**
ISBN: 1-59378-201-2

Copyright © 2003, 2005 • Kennel Club Books, LLC
308 Main Street, Allenhurst, NJ 07711 USA
Cover Design Patented: US 6,435,559 B2 • Printed in South Korea

10 9 8 7 6 5 4 3 2

One of the world's most recognizable and popular working dogs is the German Shepherd Dog, a dedicated companion and guardian.

HISTORY OF THE
GERMAN SHEPHERD DOG

"...as hounds and greyhounds,
mongrels, spaniels, curs
Shoughs, water-rugs, and
demi-wolves are clept
All by the name of dogs.
The valued file
Distinguishes the swift,
the slow, the subtle
The housekeeper, the hunter,
every one
According to the gift which
bounteous nature
Hath in him closed, whereby
he does receive
Particular addition from the bill
That writes them all alike..."
—Macbeth

HISTORY AND ORIGINAL PURPOSE IN GERMANY

The particular qualifications that set the German Shepherd Dog apart from the general catalog that lists all breeds are numerous and evident from the first moment in the history of the dog.

Considerations of companionship and domination aside, the first domesticated canines were utilized for practical and essential purposes such as the guarding and control of livestock. From the crude animals that helped early shepherds with their flocks evolved light-gaited,

German Shepherd Dogs are still used for sheep-herding and flock-guarding.

weather-impervious, dependable animals, commonly categorized as sheepdogs.

In 1891, a group of German admirers of this rugged, unrefined dog formed the Phylax Society, named after the Greek word *phylaxis,* which means "to watch over or guard." The purpose of this organization was to standardize the varied collection of sheepherding dogs into a breed of native German dog with a fixed appearance and character.

The Phylax Society lasted until only 1894, but its purpose and vision were continued in the person of one man, Max Emil Friedrich von Stephanitz, consid-ered by many to be the single greatest force in the establishment of the German Shepherd Dog as a pure breed.

The originator of the breed was discovered by von Stephanitz on April 3, 1899, when he and another sheepdog enthusiast were attending an exhibition of these herding dogs. The dog they encountered was agile, powerful, alert and strongly adapted to his utilitarian purpose. To von Stephanitz, this particular animal seemed to be the perfect embodiment of the worker and guardian ideal that he held for this type of dog. The overt intelligence and desire to serve apparent in the

In 1891 the development of the German Shepherd began. Its objective was to produce a German dog with a standard appearance and behavior.

Because the well-trained German Shepherd Dog is so eager to please his master (or mistress), he has been utilized in a variety of roles.

dog's temperament belied his wild, wolfish appearance. Von Stephanitz bought the dog on the spot. His original name, Hektor von Linksrhein, was changed to Horand von Grafrath and he was registered as German Shepherd Dog, S.Z. 1, the first entry in von Stephanitz's new organization, *Verein für Deutsche Schäferhunde.* This was the beginning of the national German dog club known as the S.V., the largest individual breed club in the world.

Horand proved to be an able stud and the traits that von Stephanitz prized upon first meeting the dog were passed on to succeeding dogs and strengthened by this early breeder's careful policies of inbreeding, called linebreeding, a practice that seeks to emphasize and strengthen desirable characteristics through determined genetic management in the kennel and farm.

Always foremost in von Stephanitz's mind was the working, practical ideal of the breed. From the beginning, form in the German Shepherd Dog was not intended to deviate from function. Von Stephanitz foresaw an early threat to the breed's validity as working animals when human society passed from a largely agricultural and agrarian basis to an industrialized economy. As a first step, he persuaded the German government to accept the breed

Despite the surges and declines in the breed's popularity throughout history, today the German Shepherd is one of the most beloved breeds in the world.

Kennel-Club-registered German Shepherd.

The German Shepherd Dog Club of America took root in 1913, planted by B. H. Throop of Pennsylvania and Anne Tracy of New Jersey. By 1916, the Club was incorporated and sponsored its first specialty show, which boasted an entry of 40 dogs. In 1918, the German Shepherd Dog Club of America inaugurated the title of Grand Champion (changed to Grand Victor (males)

for police work. This was the beginning of the breed's association with law enforcement and military use. Soon the German Shepherd's qualities of intelligence, reliability and hardiness, the central aspects of its character and existence in history, secured its use in many important roles, the most noble of which is the dog's role as a guide for the blind.

WORLD-WIDE HURDLES FOR THE BREED

The first German Shepherd Dog to come to America was imported by Otto Gross in 1905. Bred by P. Stretter, Mira of Dalmore was exhibited in the Miscellaneous Class and won ribbons. Mira's impact on the breed is merely anecdotal and she was neither registered nor bred. Queen of Switzerland, owned by Adolph Vogt, was the first American-

POPULARITY

It was not until after the war that the breed recaptured American favor, based this time upon its time-old qualities of service and intelligence. Many American soldiers returned from Europe with stories of the courage and reliability of the dogs that they had seen in military and Red Cross service. Many also returned with the dogs themselves. This growing popularity was accelerated by two famous silent film heroes, who happened to be German Shepherd Dogs, Rin Tin Tin and Strongheart.

The original Rin Tin Tin was brought to the United States by a returned soldier. The dog lived for only 13 years but others of the breed carried forward the name and role. Strongheart, equally popular at the time but less known today, was a fully trained police dog imported to America for work in the movie industry.

and Grand Victrix (females) in 1925) for winners at the national specialty. Any dog with this prefix has won either Best of Breed or Best of Opposite Sex. The first dogs to earn the title, in 1918, were Komet v. Hohelfut and Lotte v. Edelweis. The first dog to win the title multiple times was Ch. Arko v. Sadowaberg (who won it in 1927, 1928, 1929 and 1931). He was owned by Jessaford Kennels.

The first two champions were Lux (owned by Anne Tracy) and Herta von Ehrangrund (owned by L. I. De Winter). The importation of Apollo von Hunenstein from Germany had a lasting impact on the breed, as this famous Conti-

nental winner brought quality and style to the American lines. He was imported by B. H. Throop and was a popular sire, having attained the American Grand Victor title in 1919. Among the first Best in Show winners was another import, Dolf von Dusternbrook, a grandson of Apollo, imported by the Joselle Kennels.

Worthy of special note during the pre-World War I period is breeder John Gans of Staten Island, who imported and bred dozens of magnificent champions, some of which were from the Flora Berkemeyer Kennels. Of course, the war took a toll on the breed, as it did all breeds, espe-

The German Shepherd's character is evident in his noble expression.

cially those of German descent. The breed became known as "Shepherd Dogs" or "Police Dogs" in the US, as it became known as "Alsatian Wolf Dogs" in the UK during World War II. The post-World War I recovery period of the breed, inaugurated by returning American soldiers with Shepherd puppies, and Hollywood's idolization of the breed (in *Rin Tin Tin* and *Strongheart*) blossomed as swiftly as the popularity had dissipated when the war began.

Although derived from German stock, the breed members in the US today are all-American.

The Hamilton Farm Kennels made German Shepherd history in the 1920s with a number of handsome dogs, including Grand Victor Champion Erich von Grafenwerth and Anni von Humboldtpark. Erich was a prized sire and show dog, later sold to Giralda Farms of the famous Geraldine Rockefeller Dodge, whose association with the breed and the dog fancy in the US is significant and historical. It was Mrs. Dodge's vision that the Morris and Essex

Kennel Club Show take place on her estate grounds, and in its day the show was the most spectacular of American shows. She also imported remarkable bitches and developed a unique line of homebred champions. The Giralda Shepherds had a lasting impact on the breed and were a force in the show ring for 30 years.

It is impossible to trace all of the important breeders in the US, as there have been dozens and dozens. Kennels like Ruthland, San Miguel, Long Worth, Villa Marina, Grafmar, Ralston, Jeff-Lynne and Liebestraum left their indelible mark on the breed through the 1950s, producing top show dogs and breeding stock. These early kennels laid the foundation for the breeders who followed.

The modern history of the breed is laden with Best in Show winners and prolific sires and dams, far too many to list. We would be remiss not to mention two quintessential Shepherds who have made recent history. Covy Tucker Hill has the distinction of producing the first (and only) German Shepherd Dog to win the Westminster Kennel Club, Champion Covy Tucker Hill Manhattan, owned by Jane A. Firestone and Shirlee Braunstein. Manhattan won this award in 1987. Another Covy Tucker

Hill dog owned by Mrs. Firestone is noted for making breed history as the number-one show dog of all-time, Ch. Altana's Mystique, a popular bitch handled by Jimmy Moses. Mystique retired with 494 Best of Breed awards and 274 Best in Show wins. Although she never won the Westminster show (she won Group One twice), she should have!

In the US today, the German Shepherd remains a popular

TO THE RESCUE

Most pure-bred dog fancies reach out to abandoned and abused members of their particular breed, and the German Shepherd fraternity is no different. As a part of the German Shepherd Dog Club of America, the American German Shepherd Rescue Association, Inc. was developed to safeguard the breed from cruelty, abandonment and other types of neglect. The organization raises funds to operate a number of worthy projects, including the Help Line Referral Network, which maintains a directory of rescue services in America; a grant service, which helps fund smaller breed rescue operations; the distribution of information and guidelines for rescue and the dissemination of educational materials.

choice for Best in Show as well as a spectacular obedience, herding, tracking and agility contender. Likewise, the breed continues to rank in the top five AKC breeds, with over 50,000 dogs registered annually. The German Shepherd Dog Club of America is proud that many breed members continue to be of service to humankind, as service dogs for the blind and deaf, as protection dogs and military dogs and as search-and-rescue dogs. Many brave Shepherds assisted rescue workers in New York City at Ground Zero, working side by side for nine months after those hateful attacks.

Historically speaking, it was the hard work and noble effort of these dogs in various military and life-saving capacities that renewed admiration and avid acceptance of the German Shepherd, a breed that today enjoys unprecedented, uninterrupted popularity. So intense became the demand for this breed that unscrupulous and uncontrolled breeding led to many medical and behavioral problems, most notably hip dysplasia, which continue to plague the breed today. Over-breeding also led to the fear biters and other neurotic specimens that threatened the reputation of this normally noble and kind dog.

During the 1960s, veterinarians and protectors of the breed, most prominently the German Shepherd Dog Club of America and the German S.V., joined together to control these problems and to safeguard this breed of guardians. For example, today there is a radiological method of determining hip dysplasia in individual dogs and certifying those free of the condition as dogs of breeding quality.

The American club has affixed a Register of Merit, or ROM, title to dogs whose offspring prove healthy and worthy of showing. The S.V. has created Class I (dogs with no fault) and Class II (dogs with minor faults) rankings to underscore and protect the ideals of physical and mental soundness that were established by the architects of the breed.

Reputable breeders have followed suit to ensure the health, temperament and popularity of the breed. They not only scrutinize the backgrounds of sires and dams but also interrogate buyers about how they intend to raise and use their puppies.

The modern German Shepherd Dog has weathered a difficult and varied history, with the features that set it apart from and above other breeds intact and zealously protected. It is fitting that the qualities of nobility and protection that brought these canine and human companions first together should continue to characterize their association.

American
breeders strive
to produce
sound and intel-
ligent German
Shepherds, free
from hereditary
diseases.

Since its beginnings, the German Shepherd Dog has evolved into one of the most desirable breeds. Puppies from properly bred, healthy parents are avidly sought after.

CHARACTERISTICS OF THE
GERMAN SHEPHERD DOG

Those who are considering sharing a significant portion of their lives with a German Shepherd Dog will do well to discount the associations, good or bad, that have become attached to the dog throughout its intricate history and to concentrate upon the qualities and characteristics that first attracted von Stephanitz to the animal. The original and, in this case, ideal German Shepherd

Counted among the most trainable of all pure-bred dogs, the German Shepherd excels in numerous forums of service and competition.

Dog was agile, powerful, rugged, steady, alert and intelligent. Above all, the dog delighted in work and purpose. This dog's association with man was neither servile nor amusing, nor was the dog ever intended to be an object of beauty. The German Shepherd Dog began on a footing as equal to man as a canine ever achieved.

Such nobility of purpose perhaps cannot be sustained in the ordinary households that will be home to the vast majority of German Shepherd Dogs, but the ideal should neither be forgotten nor ignored. Expect that you and your German Shepherd Dog will be equal on some intrinsic level and your relationship will be well founded.

HOW BIG SHOULD THE SHEPHERD BE?

Originally intended for herding, German Shepherd Dogs were medium-sized, but as guarding and other uses became predominant, the breed became progressively larger. Today adult males are 24–26 inches at the withers and females are approximately 2 inches smaller. The normal weight range is 66–88 lbs. Adult physical characteristics are achieved by 10–18 months, but dogs will typically fill out until three years of age. Large size is not necessarily preferred and may, in some cases, exacerbate the tendency to certain orthopedic disorders.

The all-weather coat of the German Shepherd does not require much time from his owner. This handsome dog has a fairly short coat.

PHYSICAL CHARACTERISTICS

Puppies have floppy ears that stand erect by six or seven months of age. Some dogs have ears that never stand. Although taping most often can correct this fault, these dogs should be considered poor choices for breeding.

Conventional depictions of the breed emphasize the black and tan coloring with saddleback markings, but the German Shepherd Dog comes in a wide variety of colors such as black and red, black and cream, all black, all white, sable (with various colorations), black and silver, liver and blue. Breeders do not favor the white, liver or blue varieties; the AKC lists white dogs among the disqualifications.

Coats are double, with the coarser outer coat serving to resist water and debris, and the soft dense undercoat working to retain body heat during cold seasons. The fur can range from short and coarse to long and soft. Long-coated dogs, however, are not eligible for showing in the breed ring.

German Shepherd Dogs will shed all year long, with heavy shedding during the spring and fall. Grooming, however, is not difficult. Regular light brushing is all that is required. Bathing, when necessary, should employ a hypoallergenic shampoo.

The main concern of every admirer of the German Shepherd Dog, however, is character. The animal should be courageous, intelligent, playful and safe with children and obedient and responsive to his owner. These elements of sound disposition and utility supersede any and all physical ideals.

PERSONALITY

Throughout history, in whatever capacity the German Shepherd has been used, one thing that has been constant is the bond that has developed between the dogs and their owners. Since the dogs have traditionally been used as service and working dogs, this bond was a necessity. The dogs had to be very obedient and very reliable to perform their given tasks. Since a major role of the German Shepherd has been that of a guard dog, the dogs also had to be very protective of their owners. These characteristics translate into a pet dog that is very intelligent, highly trainable and extremely loyal. The pet German Shepherd watches over the entire family and seems

BEHAVIOR & PERSONALITY

The behavior and personality of your German Shepherd Dog will reflect your care and training more than any other breed characteristics. Remember that these dogs require a purposeful existence, so plan your relationship around activities that serve this most basic and important need. All the good potential of the breed will naturally follow.

to be able to sense if someone is in trouble or needs help. Likewise, the German Shepherd is a wonderful protector of children and of his owner's property.

Due to these protective instincts, the German Shepherd is naturally wary of strangers. This is not to say that he is not a friendly dog, but he chooses whom to befriend based on his owner's attitude. "Any friend of yours is a friend of mine," the German Shepherd seems to say to his owner, and he fiercely trusts his owner's judgment. The dog will warm up to people that he becomes familiar with; he looks to his owner for clues about who is okay and who is not. Proper socialization and introduction to people from an early age are necessary to help the German Shepherd become more accepting of the people he meets.

The German Shepherd is noble and proud—he has a lot going for him and he knows it! A wonderful combination of stamina, athleticism, intelligence, grace and beauty, he personifies the virtues of "man's best friend."

OWNER SUITABILITY

Because the German Shepherd Dog is so devoted to his owner, it is only natural that he should thrive best with an owner who can show him equal devotion. The German Shepherd basks in his owner's attention. It is not necessarily true that the only type of person suitable to own a German Shepherd is one who is home all day, but the owner who spends the day at work must plan on time with the dog upon his return home.

Exercise is also a consideration for the German Shepherd. Remember, these dogs were bred to work and to be active. The breeders' original focus was on function. Since the pet dog is not being used for his intended purpose, he must be active in other ways. A German Shepherd who lives at home with his owner cannot exercise himself; it is something that both dog and owner need to participate in. It is not fair to the dog, who has patiently waited all day for his owner to return from work, for the owner to come home and promptly park himself on the couch for the remainder of the evening. Exercise is essential for the German Shepherd's well-being, both physically and mentally. It provides this athletic breed with much-needed activity, plus it helps him feel like he has a purpose.

Zwinger von Muldental and his young friend keep watch over the property.

A house with a securely fenced-in yard is ideal for a German Shepherd owner, as the dog will have some freedom to run and play by himself. The dog should still be under the owner's supervision when off-leash, but at least the dog will not be totally dependent on his owner for exercise. This does not make up for time spent with his owner, but will at least give the dog some physical benefits. An owner who keeps a German Shepherd in a house without a yard or in an apartment must make the commitment to regular runs/walks/ playtime with the dog.

The German Shepherd will fit into just about any family structure...adults, children, single people, etc. It is just necessary that the breed's characteristics are taken into consideration.

VERSATILITY AND AGILITY

Although your German Shepherd Dog may never be required to do more than provide companionship and protection to you and your family, you should be proud to consider the many functions that the breed can be called upon to perform.

MILITARY DOGS
German Shepherd Dogs have been used as military dogs since World War I. Their roles have been numerous. The dogs served as sentries, guards, mine detectors, rescuers of wounded soldiers and carriers of food and medicine.

The instinct to serve, which is born in the animal, is the foundation of his functional versatility along with his physical and mental traits of strength, size, endurance and intelligence. It would be fair to say that the majority of all service dogs in the world are German Shepherd Dogs. The potential for specific service duties lies within each German Shepherd Dog, but professional training is required to actualize it in almost every case.

As previously noted, the German Shepherd Dog is an excellent herding dog. This was his original function and remains a central factor in his modern versatility. The dog's endurance, his rough-coated imperviousness to weather, his sure-footed speed, responsiveness and his deep-rooted instinct to protect anything small or weak make him an ideal herding choice.

It is only in Germany, however, that the German Shepherd Dog is a first choice among farmers and stock owners. In the United States and Great Britain, other native breeds, more traditional and therefore more attractive to some, like the Australian Shepherd and the Border Collie, are predominantly seen in herding capacities.

German Shepherd Dogs were especially impressive as scout dogs, often able to detect the presence of an enemy at 100 yards away. Countless human lives were saved by these dogs but many of the animals were sacrificed in services like mine detection.

From these military uses developed the breed's important

role as police dogs. In the pursuit and apprehension of criminals, the breed has proven itself valuable and rather more effective, certainly more humane, than guns. The dog's cool nerves and intelligence make him an excellent choice for crowd control. His scenting ability makes him invaluable in search-and-rescue work, as well as bomb and drug detection.

The skills and abilities of these functions are combined in *Schutzhund*, a training and competition program that emphasizes the elements of protection. Schutzhund means "protection dog" in German. Schutzhund trials have existed since the early 1900s. They include tests for temperament, tracking and protection. Dogs are scored according to their performance in these areas and must exhibit complete obedience (despite distraction), confidence, courage, scenting ability, determination and concentration in tracking.

The preceding roles have stressed obedience founded upon the breed's natural proclivities.

Excelling in police work, the German Shepherd Dog has earned the highest accolades. Winning Police Dog Action is Overhills Foggarty, bred by Meg Purnell-Carpenter and handled by WPC Leigh White.

SCHUTZHUND DOGS

In Schutzhund trials, dogs are rated by performance and can earn the titles of SchH. I (beginner), SchH. II (intermediate) and SchH. III (master). These titles can be appended to the dog's name and pedigree.

The German Shepherd Dog is not a particularly aggressive dog. He is, however, very protective of his family and property. This is the basis of the alertness and protective instinct that have made him a staple in institutional use and an effective watchdog for the home and family.

The most noble and pride-provoking use of the German Shepherd Dog has been in the service of people with physical challenges. The German Shepherd Dog was the first dog used as a guide dog for blind individuals and later for deaf individuals. The

If you are seeking a top-rate protection dog, then select a puppy from proven stock. Both of these police dogs were bred by Meg Purnell-Carpenter.

dog's initial employment as guides for blind World War I veterans led to the creation of the Seeing Eye® Foundation in 1929. Today this breed's traits of composure, intelligence and responsibility, combined with all of his other excellent aspects, continue to make him the first choice in this role and all of the other roles designed to serve humankind.

In recent years, hip dysplasia has declined in incidence in the breed. This x-ray shows perceptible hip dysplasia in a German Shepherd Dog, which must be treated as soon as possible.

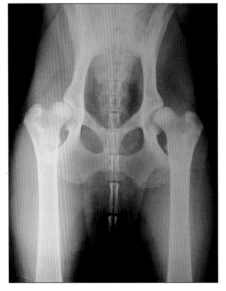

SHEPHERD SERVICE

The German Shepherd Dog has been used in more areas of service to humankind than any other breed. Here are ten important areas that the breed has served:

1. Police and military work.
2. Herding livestock for farms and ranches.
3. Guides for the blind.
4. Hearing dogs for the deaf.
5. Arson and bomb detection.
6. Drug and substance detection.
7. Guard dogs for businesses and residences.
8. Search-and-rescue/avalanche, disaster and earthquake work.
9. Therapy dogs for hospitals.
10. Cancer detection.

HEALTH CONSIDERATIONS AND HEREDITARY DISEASES

Given the care that love and respect for the animal demand, the German Shepherd Dog is a tough and healthy breed. It has been frequently stressed here that the German Shepherd Dog was, from his earliest history, developed as a working animal and, therefore, frequent and, above all, purposeful activity is essential to his health. Without regular exercise and activity, the breed is foremost susceptible to rheumatism, the symptoms of which are similar to those seen in humans: swelling and stiffening of the affected joints and pain in movement. Because some of the symptoms of this condition are shared by the far more serious hip dysplasia, prompt professional attention is necessary when symptoms are first displayed.

Skin problems are also frequent in the breed. Slow, constant scratching, as opposed to the short burst of scratching associated with fleas, is a sign of skin trouble. If observed early, the majority of these problems can be reduced quickly by veterinary care and diet.

Other diseases and conditions found in the German Shepherd Dogs are not exclusive to the breed but are shared by others of its various type. Because, for example, the German Shepherd Dog is a large breed, it is affected by osteochondritis dissecans, panosteitis, hypertrophic osteodystrophy and myasthenia gravis, all diseases of the bone.

Because of his shepherding nature, the German Shepherd Dog is prone to the eye conditions typical of this category of dog like Collie eye, pannus, cataracts and retinal dysplasia.

Epilepsy is another condition that affects shepherding dogs. Blood conditions like von Willebrand's disease and hemophilia A, and heart problems such as patent or persistent ductus arteriosis and persistent right aortic arch, are problems that affect most canines and the German Shepherd Dog is not excluded.

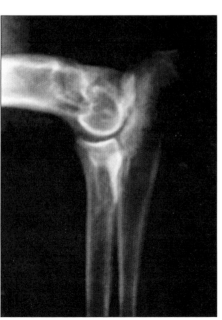 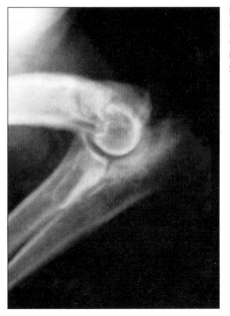

Elbow dysplasia in a three-and-a-half-year-old male German Shepherd Dog.

No discussion of health concerning the German Shepherd Dog can end, however, without more detailed talk about hip dysplasia (HD). German Shepherd Dogs have the highest percentage rate of HD of any breed. The fact that it stands to reason that the most popular and excessively bred dog should most reveal this hereditary condition does nothing to ameliorate the seriousness of the problem.

Dysplastic dogs have incorrectly developed hip joints that are prone to arthritis and are wildly painful. These dogs are unable to work or even move without discomfort. Breeders and veterinarians continue to study this condition and guard against its occurrence, but it is the responsibility of every prospective German Shepherd Dog owner to know that the parents and grandparents of his puppy had hips rated good or better.

It is possible that part of the breed's predisposition to this condition may have been caused by the early developer's exaggeration of the powerful downward curve of the animals' posture. If true, it is sad that the unassailable, largely unchanged character of this noble breed should be linked to this weakness, unknowingly fostered by its earliest architects.

More recently, elbow dysplasia has become a concern and screening criteria have also been developed. Those genetic physical problems to which the breed is heir are considerations that are best countered by careful planning and care in the choice and selection of breeder and animal.

Although the list of congenital diseases to which German Shepherd Dogs are prone is somewhat daunting, most representatives of the breed are healthy indeed. Many Shepherds can live heartily past ten years of age, and some have been known to be exuberant teenagers. Since the German Shepherd by nature is an active working dog, good health and soundness, both physical and mental, is an absolute necessity for all breed members.

When selecting your German Shepherd puppy, do not shop for convenience and do not be thrifty. You deserve to have the best dog that your money can buy. A well-bred Shepherd from quality stock (lines that have been tested for hereditary problems for generations) is your best choice. Even though a Shepherd with only mild dysplasia can still lead a normal life, no one wants to see his best friend compromised in any fashion. It is strongly recommended that you, as a potential owner, thoroughly investigate your puppy before purchase, so that your heart is not shattered by adopting a lovely dog with serious health problems.

BREED STANDARD FOR THE
GERMAN SHEPHERD DOG

WHAT IS A BREED STANDARD?
A breed standard is a guide that breeders use to develop their breeding programs and judges use to evaluate dogs in a conformation show. It is a written "blueprint" of the ideal German Shepherd Dog. The standard was drawn up by the national breed club, the German Shepherd Dog Club of America, and then submitted to the American Kennel Club, the governing body of pure-bred dogs in the US, for acceptance.

The head to tail portrait of the German Shepherd Dog will be revealed in the following description, which is excerpted from the American Kennel Club standard.

The breed standard describes the perfect German Shepherd Dog, and all show dogs are compared to this ideal.

THE AMERICAN KENNEL CLUB STANDARD FOR THE GERMAN SHEPHERD DOG

General Appearance: The first impression of a good German Shepherd Dog is that of a strong, agile, well muscled animal, alert and full of life. It is well balanced, with harmonious development of the forequarter and hindquarter. The dog is longer than tall, deep-bodied, and presents an outline of smooth curves rather than angles. It looks substantial and not spindly, giving the impression, both at rest and in motion, of muscular fitness and nimbleness without any look of clumsiness or soft living. The ideal dog is stamped with a look of quality and nobility—difficult to define, but unmistakable when present.

The German Shepherd's eyes should be almond-shaped and brown in color. This Shepherd has the desirable self-assured and alert expression.

Temperament: The breed has a distinct personality marked by direct and fearless, but not hostile, expression, self-confidence and a certain aloofness that does not lend itself to immediate and indiscriminate friendships. The dog must be approachable, quietly standing its ground and showing confidence and willingness to meet overtures without itself making them. It is poised, but when the occasion demands, eager and alert; both fit and willing to serve in its capacity as companion, watchdog, blind leader, herding dog, or guardian, whichever the circumstances may demand. Lack of confidence under any surroundings is not typical of good character. The ideal dog is a working animal with an incorruptible character combined with body and gait suitable for the arduous work that constitutes its primary purpose.

Size, Proportion, Substance: The desired height for males at the top of the highest point of the shoulder blade is 24 to 26 inches; and for bitches, 22 to 24 inches. The German Shepherd Dog is longer than tall, with the most desirable proportion as 10 to 8.5. The desirable long proportion is not derived from a long back, but from overall length with relation to height, which is achieved by length of forequarter and length of withers and hindquarter, viewed from the side.

Head: The head is noble, cleanly chiseled, strong without coarseness, but above all not fine, and in proportion to the body. The head of the male is distinctly masculine, and that of the bitch distinctly feminine.

The expression keen, intelligent and composed. Eyes of medium size, almond shaped, set a little obliquely and not protruding. The color is as dark as possible. Ears are moderately pointed, in proportion to the skull, open toward the front, and carried erect when at attention, the ideal carriage being one in which the center lines of the ears, viewed from the front, are parallel to each other and perpendicular to the ground. A dog with cropped or hanging ears must be disqualified.

Seen from the front the forehead is only moderately arched, and the skull slopes into the long, wedge-shaped muzzle without abrupt stop. The muzzle is long and strong, and its topline is parallel to the topline of the skull. Nose black. Teeth—42 in number—20 upper and 22 lower—are strongly developed and meet in a scissors bite in

Longer than tall, the German Shepherd does not possess a long back but rather length in the fore- and hindquarters.

MEETING THE IDEAL

The American Kennel Club defines a standard as: "A description of the ideal dog of each recognized breed, to serve as an ideal against which dogs are judged at shows." This "blueprint" is drawn up by the breed's recognized parent club, approved by a majority of its membership and then submitted to the AKC for approval. The AKC states that "An understanding of any breed must begin with its standard. This applies to all dogs, not just those intended for showing." The picture that the standard draws of the dog's type, gait, temperament and structure is the guiding image used by breeders as they plan their programs.

which part of the inner surface of the upper incisors meet and engage part of the outer surface of the lower incisors.

Neck, Topline, Body: The neck is strong and muscular, clean-cut and relatively long, proportionate in size to the head and without loose folds of skin. When the dog is at attention or excited, the head is raised and the neck carried high; otherwise typical carriage of the head is forward rather than up and but little higher than the top of the shoulders, particularly in motion.

Topline— The withers are higher than and sloping into the level back. The back is straight, very strongly developed without sag or roach, and relatively short. The whole structure of the body gives an impression of depth and solidity without bulkiness.

Chest—Commencing at the prosternum, it is well filled and carried well down between the legs. It is deep and capacious, never shallow, with ample room for lungs and heart, carried well forward, with the prosternum showing ahead of the shoulder in profile. Ribs well sprung and long, neither barrel-shaped nor too flat, and carried down to a sternum which reaches to the elbows. Abdomen firmly held and not paunchy. The bottom line is only moderately tucked up in the loin.

Loin—Viewed from the top, broad and strong. Croup long and gradually sloping. Tail bushy, with the last vertebra extended at least to the hock joint. It is set smoothly into the croup and low rather than high. At rest, the tail hangs in a slight curve like a saber. When the dog is excited or in motion, the curve is accentuated and the tail raised, but it should never be curled forward beyond a vertical line.

Forequarters: The shoulder blades are long and obliquely angled, laid on flat and not placed forward. The upper arm joins the shoulder blade at about a right angle. Both the upper arm and the shoulder blade are well muscled. The forelegs, viewed from all sides, are straight and the bone oval rather than round. The pasterns are strong and springy and angulated at approximately a 25-degree angle from the vertical. Dewclaws on the forelegs may be removed, but are normally left on. The feet are short, compact with toes well arched, pads thick and firm, nails short and dark.

Hindquarters: The whole assembly of the thigh, viewed from the side, is broad, with both upper and lower thigh well muscled, forming as nearly as possible a right angle. The upper thigh bone parallels the shoulder

The German Shepherd should be deep-bodied and appear smoothly curved, not angular. The stamp of quality and nobility, once recognized, is unmistakable.

	CORRECT	**INCORRECT**

EARS
Should be held erect, moderately pointed and open toward the front.

BITE
Teeth should meet in a scissors bite, jaw should not be undershot.

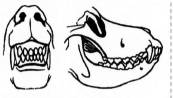

FOREQUARTERS
Forelegs should be straight from pasterns to elbows when viewed from any angle.

CROUP
Should be long and gradually sloping; should not be short, steep or flat.

HINDQUARTERS
Angulation in proportion to front angulation, with strong, short hocks, tightly articulated.

FEET
Should be short, compact with well-arched toe.

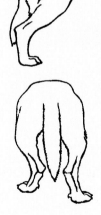

blade while the lower thigh bone parallels the upper arm. The metatarsus (the unit between the hock joint and the foot) is short, strong and tightly articulated. The dewclaws, if any, should be removed from the hind legs. Feet as in front.

Coat: The ideal dog has a double coat of medium length. The outer coat should be as dense as possible, hair straight, harsh and lying close to the body. A slightly wavy outer coat, often of wiry texture, is permissible. The head, including the inner ear and foreface, and the legs and paws are covered with short hair, and the neck with longer and thicker hair. The rear of the forelegs and hind legs has somewhat longer hair extending to the pastern and hock, respectively. Faults in coat include soft, silky, too long outer coat, woolly, curly, and open coat.

Color: The German Shepherd Dog varies in color, and most colors are permissible. Strong rich colors

It's hard to determine a young pup's show potential. It's best to evaluate his conformation after he has gone through the awkward stages of growth.

are preferred. Pale, washed-out colors and blues or livers are serious faults. A white dog must be disqualified.

Gait: A German Shepherd Dog is a trotting dog, and its structure has been developed to meet the requirements of its work.

General Impression— The gait is outreaching, elastic, seemingly without effort, smooth and rhythmic, covering the maximum amount of ground with the minimum number of steps. At a walk it covers a great deal of ground, with long stride of both hind legs and forelegs. At a trot the dog covers still more ground with even longer stride, and moves powerfully but easily, with coordination and balance so that the gait appears to be the steady motion of a well-lubricated machine.

DISQUALIFICATIONS
- Cropped or hanging ears.
- Dogs with noses not predominantly black.
- Undershot jaw.
- Docked tail.
- White dogs.
- Any dog that attempts to bite the judge.

A well-bred German Shepherd is a sight to behold. Look for a healthy, alert pup to grow into a faithful guardian and companion.

GERMAN SHEPHERD DOG

OWNER CONSIDERATIONS

Although the reader of these pages may be more likely interested in finding a companion and family animal than a show champion or working dog, there remain many serious factors governing your choice. A primary consideration is time, not only the time of the animal's allotted lifespan, which is well over ten years, but also the time required for the owner to exercise and care for the creature. If you are not committed to the welfare and whole existence of this energetic, purposeful animal; if, in the simplest, most basic example, you are not willing to walk your

All German Shepherd puppies are lovable dogs. Don't let your heart make the selection...use your head.

dog daily, despite the weather, do not choose a German Shepherd Dog as a companion.

Space is another important consideration. The German Shepherd Dog in early puppyhood may be well accommodated in a corner of your kitchen but after only six months, when the dog is likely over 60 pounds, more space certainly will be required. A yard with a fence is also a basic and reasonable expectation.

Along with these factors, there are the usual problems associated with puppies of any breed like the damages likely to be sustained by your floors, furniture, garden and, not least of all, restrictions to your freedom (of movement), as in vacations or weekend trips. This union is a serious affair and

PUPPY APPEARANCE

Your puppy should have a well-fed appearance but not a distended abdomen, which may indicate worms or incorrect feeding, or both. The body should be firm, with a solid feel. The skin of the abdomen should be pale pink and clean, without signs of scratching or rash. The dewclaws on the forelegs are traditionally left on. Check the hind legs to make certain that dewclaws were removed, if any were present at birth.

should be deeply considered. Once decided, though, your choice of a German Shepherd Dog is, perhaps, the most rewarding of all breeds. A few suggestions will help in the purchase of your dog.

ACQUIRING A PUPPY
The best method of obtaining your puppy is to seek out a reputable breeder. This is suggested even if you are not looking for a show specimen. The novice breeders and pet owners who advertise at attractive prices in the local newspapers are probably kind enough towards their dogs, but perhaps do not have the expertise or facilities required to successfully raise these demanding animals. These pet puppies are frequently badly weaned and left with the mother too long without the supplemental feeding required by this fast-growing breed. This lack of proper feeding can lead to indigestion, rickets, weak bones, poor teeth and other problems. Veterinary bills may soon distort initial savings into financial or, worse, emotional loss.

Inquire about inoculations and when the puppy was last dosed for worms. Check the ears. Although many puppies do not have erect ears until five or six months, some movement forward and signs of lifting when the puppy is alerted are good predictors of normal development.

Color is a matter of personal choice, but whatever color you prefer, your puppy should have a dark nose and, preferably, dark toenails. This is a consideration of

PEDIGREE AND REGISTRATION CERTIFICATE
Too often new owners are confused between these two important documents. Your puppy's pedigree, essentially a family tree, is a written record of a dog's genealogy of three generations or more. The pedigree will show you the names as well as performance titles of all of the dogs in your pup's background. Your breeder must provide you with a registration application, with his part properly filled out. You must complete the application and send it to the American Kennel Club (AKC) with the proper fee. The seller must provide you with complete records to identify the puppy. The AKC requires that the seller provide the buyer with the following: breed; sex, color and markings; date of birth; litter number (when available); names and registration numbers of the parents; breeder's name; and date sold or delivered.

pigmentation, which should not be confused with color. Color in German Shepherd Dogs generally becomes lighter, so it is wise to choose a puppy with deep rich pigmentation and as much black as possible. Dark eyes are best in any color. Look for expression in your puppy's eyes, as this is a good sign of intelligence.

Note the way your choice moves. The German Shepherd Dog, even in puppyhood, should show light and swift movement with no tendency to stumble or drag the hind feet. Look at the mouth to make sure that the bite is fairly even, although maturity can often correct errors present at puppyhood. If you have any doubts, ask to see the parents' mouths. This brings up an important point—do not purchase a puppy without first seeing at least one of the parents.

The choice of which sex to acquire is largely a matter of personal preference. Male dogs of this breed are equally devoted and loyal but have the drawback of being in season all year if not neutered and, therefore, prone to possible wandering. This is the central reason why females are always chosen as guide dogs for the blind.

COMMITMENT OF OWNERSHIP
After considering all of these factors, you have most likely already made some very

BOY OR GIRL?
An important consideration to be discussed is the sex of your puppy. For a family companion, a bitch may be the better choice, considering the female's inbred concern for all young creatures and her accompanying tolerance and patience. It is always advisable to spay (female) or neuter (male) a pet, which may guarantee your dog a longer life.

important decisions about selecting your puppy. You have chosen the German Shepherd, which means that you have decided which characteristics you want in a dog and what type of dog will best fit into your family and lifestyle. If you have selected a breeder, you have gone a step further—you have done your research and found a responsible, conscientious person who breeds quality German Shepherds and who should become a reliable source of help as you and your puppy adjust to life together. If you have observed a litter in action, you have gotten a firsthand

Bred for service to mankind, these two German Shepherds will pursue a career with the police. Fortunately they have an excellent start, having been bred by Meg Purnell-Carpenter of Overhill Kennels in the UK.

look at the dynamics of a puppy "pack" and, thus, you have gotten to learn about each pup's individual personality—perhaps you have even found one that particularly appeals to you.

However, even if you have not yet found the German Shepherd puppy of your dreams, observing pups will help you learn to recognize certain behavior and to determine what a pup's behavior indicates about his temperament. You will be able to pick out which pups are the leaders, which ones are less outgoing, which ones are confident, which ones are shy, friendly, aggressive, etc. Equally as important, you will learn to recognize what a healthy

pup should look and act like. All of these things will help you in your search, and when you find the German Shepherd that was meant for you, you will know it!

Researching your breed, selecting a responsible breeder and observing as many pups as possible are all important steps

QUALITY FOOD

The cost of food must be mentioned. All dogs need a good-quality food with an adequate supply of protein to develop their bones and muscles properly. Most dogs are not picky eaters but, unless fed properly, can quickly succumb to skin problems.

on the way to dog ownership. It may seem like a lot of effort...and you have not even brought the pup home yet! Remember, though, you cannot be too careful when it comes to deciding on the type of dog you want and finding out about your prospective pup's background. Buying a puppy is not—or *should* not be—a whimsical purchase. In fact, this is one instance in which you actually *do* get to choose your own family! But, you may be thinking, buying a puppy should be fun—it should not be so serious and so much work. If you keep in mind the thought that your puppy is not a cuddly stuffed toy or decorative lawn ornament, but instead will become a real member of your family, you will realize that while buying a puppy is a pleasurable and exciting endeavor, it is not something to be taken lightly. Relax...the fun will start when the pup comes home!

Always keep in mind that a puppy is nothing more than a baby in a furry disguise...a baby who is virtually helpless in a human world and who trusts his owner for fulfillment of his basic needs for survival. That goes beyond food, water and shelter; your pup needs care, protection, guidance and love. If you are not prepared to commit to this, then you are not ready to own a dog.

Your dog should be able to stand comfortably in his crate. This crate is not tall enough, especially since this young German Shepherd still has growing to do.

"Wait a minute," you say. "How hard could this be? All of my neighbors own dogs and they seem to be doing just fine. Why should I have to worry about all of this?" Well, you should not worry about it; in fact, you will probably find that once your German Shepherd pup gets used to his new home, he will fall into his place in the family quite naturally. But it never hurts to emphasize the commitment of dog ownership. With some time and patience, it is really not too difficult to raise a pup to become a well-adjusted adult dog—a dog that could be your most loyal friend.

depend on how much freedom the dog will be allowed: will he be confined to one room or a specific area in the house, or will he be allowed to roam as he pleases? Will he spend most of his time in the house or will he be primarily an outdoor dog? Whatever you decide, you must ensure that he has a place that he can "call his own."

When you bring your new puppy into your home, you are bringing him into what will become his home as well. Obviously, you did not buy a puppy so that he could take control of your house, but in order

Watching a litter in action, such as during play or at mealtimes, will tell you a lot about each pup's personality and which one is best suited to you.

PREPARING PUPPY'S PLACE IN YOUR HOME

Researching your breed and finding a breeder are only two aspects of the "homework" you will have to do before bringing your German Shepherd puppy home. You will also have to prepare your home and family for the new addition. Much like you would prepare a nursery for a newborn baby, you will need to designate a place in your home that will be the puppy's own. How you prepare your home will

German Shepherd puppies have strong jaws, so make sure that the toys you purchase will withstand heavy chewing.

CRATE-TRAINING TIPS

During crate training, you should partition off the section of the crate in which the pup stays. If he is given too big an area, this will hinder your training efforts. Crate training is based on the fact that a dog does not like to soil his sleeping quarters, so it is ineffective to keep a pup in a crate that is so big that he can eliminate in one end and get far enough away from it to sleep. Also, you want to make the crate den-like for the pup. Blankets and a favorite toy will make the crate cozy for the small pup; as he grows, you may want to evict some of his "roommates" to make more room. It will take some coaxing at first, but be patient. Given some time to get used to it, your pup will adapt to his new home-within-a-home quite nicely.

for a puppy to grow into a stable, well-adjusted dog, he has to feel comfortable in his surroundings. Remember, he is leaving the warmth and security of his mother and littermates, plus the familiarity of the only place he has ever known, so it is important to make his transition as easy as possible. By preparing a place in your home for the puppy, you are making him feel as welcome as possible in a strange new place. It should not take him long to get used to it, but the sudden shock of being transplanted is somewhat traumatic for a young pup. Imagine how a small child would feel in the same situation—that is how your puppy must be feeling. It is up to you to reassure him and to let him know, "Little guy, you are going to like it here."

WHAT YOU SHOULD BUY

CRATE

To someone unfamiliar with the use of crates in dog training, it may seem like punishment to shut a dog in a crate; this is not the case at all. Crates *are not* cruel—crates have many humane and highly effective uses in dog care and training. For example, crate training is the most popular and a very successful housebreaking method used by trainers today. Also, a crate can keep your dog safe during travel; and, perhaps most importantly, a crate provides

Your pet shop should have all the supplies you will require for your new German Shepherd puppy.

your dog with a place of his own in your home. It serves as a "doggie bedroom" of sorts—your German Shepherd can curl up in his crate when he wants to sleep or when he just needs a break. Many dogs sleep in their crates overnight. With a soft crate liner and a favorite toy, a crate becomes a cozy pseudo-den for your dog. Like his ancestors, he too will seek out the comfort and retreat of a den—you just happen to be providing him with something a little more luxurious than leaves and twigs lining an earthen ditch.

As far as purchasing a crate, the type that you buy is up to you. It will most likely be one of the two most popular types: wire or fiberglass. There are advantages and disadvantages to each type. For example, a wire crate is more open, allowing the air to flow through and affording the dog a view of what is going on around him, and thus good for use in the home. A fiberglass crate, however,

is sturdier and is preferred as a travel crate since it provides more protection for the dog. The size of the crate is another thing to consider. Puppies do not stay puppies forever—in fact, sometimes it seems as if they grow right before your eyes. A small-sized crate may be fine for a very young German Shepherd pup, but it will not do him much good for long! Unless you have the money and the inclination to buy a new crate every time your pup has a growth spurt, it is better to get one that will accommodate your dog both as a pup and at full size. A large crate will be necessary for a full-grown German Shepherd, who stands up to 26 inches at the shoulder.

ARE YOU PREPARED?

Unfortunately, when a puppy is bought by someone who does not take into consideration the time and attention that dog ownership requires, it is the puppy who suffers when he is either abandoned or placed in a shelter by a frustrated owner. So all of the "homework" you do in preparation for your pup's arrival will benefit you both. The more informed you are, the more you will know what to expect and the better equipped you will be to handle the ups and downs of raising a puppy. Hopefully, everyone in the household is willing to do his part in raising and caring for the pup. The anticipation of owning a dog often brings a lot of promises from excited family members: "I will walk him every day," "I will feed him," "I will housebreak him," etc., but these things take time and effort, and promises can easily be forgotten once the novelty of the new pet has worn off.

BEDDING

A crate pad or blanket in the dog's crate will make the crate more comfortable for the pup. First, the bedding will take the place of the leaves, twigs, etc., that the pup would use in the wild to make a den; the pup can make his own "burrow" in the crate. Although your pup is far removed from his den-making ancestors, the denning instinct is still a part of his genetic makeup. Second, until you bring your pup home, he has been sleeping amid the warmth of his mother and littermates, and while soft bedding is not the same as a warm, breathing body, it still provides heat and something with which to snuggle. You will want to wash your pup's bedding frequently in case he has a toileting accident.

Toys

Toys are a must for dogs of all ages, especially for curious playful pups. Puppies are the "children" of the dog world, and what child does not love toys? Chew toys provide enjoyment to both dog and owner—your dog will enjoy playing with his favorite toys, while you will enjoy the fact that they distract him from your expensive shoes and leather sofa. Puppies love to chew; in fact, chewing is a physical need for pups as they are teething, and everything looks appetizing! The full range of your possessions—from bedroom slipper to Oriental rug—are fair game in the eyes of a teething pup. Puppies are not all that discerning when it comes to finding something to literally "sink their teeth into"— everything tastes great!

Stuffed toys are another option; these are good to put in the dog's crate to give him some company. Be careful of these, though, as a pup can de-stuff one pretty quickly, and stay away from stuffed toys with small plastic eyes or parts that a pup could choke on. Similarly, squeaky toys are quite popular. There are dogs that will come running from anywhere in the house at the first sound from their favorite squeaky friend. Again, if a pup de-stuffs one of these, the small plastic squeaker inside can be dangerous if swallowed. Supervise your pup with his toys, and monitor the condition of your pup's toys carefully and get rid of any that have been chewed to the point of becoming potentially dangerous.

Be careful of natural bones, which have a tendency to splinter into sharp, dangerous pieces. Also be careful of rawhide, which after enough chewing can turn into pieces that are easy to swallow, and also watch out for the mushy mess it can turn into on your carpet.

TOYS, TOYS, TOYS!
With a big variety of dog toys available, and so many that look like they would be a lot of fun for a dog, be careful in your selection. It is amazing what a set of puppy teeth can do to an innocent-looking toy; so, obviously, safety is a major consideration. Be sure to choose the most durable products that you can find. Hard nylon bones and toys are a safe bet, and many of them are offered in different scents and flavors that will be sure to capture your dog's attention. It is always fun to play a game of fetch with your dog, and there are balls and flying discs that are specially made to withstand the wear-and-tear of dog teeth.

LEASH

A nylon leash is probably the best option as it is the most resistant to puppy teeth should your pup take a liking to chewing on his leash. Of course, this is a habit that should be nipped in the bud, but, if your pup likes to chew on his leash, he has a very slim chance of being able to chew through the strong nylon. Nylon leashes are also lightweight, which is good for a young German Shepherd who is just getting used to the idea of walking on a leash. For everyday walking and safety purposes, the nylon leash is a good choice. As your pup grows up and gets used to walking on the leash, and can do it politely, you may want to purchase a flexible leash, which allows you either to extend the length to give the dog a broader area to explore or to pull in the leash when you

want to keep him close. Of course, there are special leashes for training purposes, and specially made leather harnesses for the working and service-dog German Shepherd, but these are not necessary for routine walks. If your German Shepherd is especially strong or tends to pull on the leash, you may want to purchase something stronger, like a thick leather leash.

COLLAR

Your pup should get used to wearing a collar all the time since you will want to attach his ID tags to his collar. Also, the leash and collar go hand in hand—you have to attach the leash to something! A lightweight nylon collar will be a good choice; make sure that it fits snugly enough so that the pup cannot wriggle out of it, but loose enough so that it will not be uncomfortably tight around the pup's neck. You should be able to fit a finger in between the pup and the collar. It may take some time for your pup to get used to wearing the collar, but soon he will not even notice that it is there. Choke collars are made for training, but should only be used by an owner who knows how to use it. Owners often put these collars on backwards; a trainer or knowledgeable pet-shop clerk can demonstrate how to use it correctly. If you use a stronger

Pet shops offer many types of dog tags. Have one engraved with all of the necessary information and attach it securely to your German Shepherd's collar.

leather leash or a chain leash to walk your German Shepherd, you will need a stronger collar as well.

FOOD AND WATER BOWLS

Your pup will need two bowls, one for food and one for water. You likely will want two sets of bowls, one for inside and one for outside. Stainless steel or sturdy plastic bowls are popular choices. Plastic bowls are more chewable, but dogs tend not to chew on the steel variety, which can also be sterilized. The most important thing is to buy sturdy bowls since, again, anything is in danger of being chewed by puppy teeth and you do not want your dog to be constantly chewing apart his bowl (for his safety and for your wallet!). German Shepherd owners should put their dogs' food and water bowls on specially made elevated stands; this brings the food closer to the dog's level so he does not have to bend down as far, thus aiding his digestion and helping to guard against bloat (gastric torsion) in deep-chested dogs like the German Shepherd.

German Shepherd Dogs must *always* have water available. Obtain a water bowl and keep it clean and full of fresh water.

CLEANING SUPPLIES

Before your pup is housebroken, you will be doing a lot of cleaning. "Accidents" will occur, which is okay for now because the puppy does not know any better. All you can do is clean up any accidents— old rags, paper towels, newspapers and a safe disinfectant are good to have on hand.

BEYOND THE BASICS

The items previously discussed are the bare necessities. You will find out what else you need as you go along—grooming supplies, flea/tick protection, baby gates to partition a room, etc.—these things will vary depending on your situation. It is just important that right away you have everything you need to feed and make your German Shepherd comfortable in his first few days at home.

PUPPY-PROOFING YOUR HOME

Aside from making sure that your German Shepherd will be comfortable in your home, you also have to make sure that your home is safe for your new dog. This means

Before you bring your German Shepherd puppy home, you should purchase all of the necessary equipment. Anticipate the needs of a growing dog and be prepared!

Properly supervise your pup when he is out exploring the yard. Many plants and bushes can be dangerous to a young pup.

taking precautions to make sure that your pup will not get into anything he should not get into and that there is nothing within his reach that may harm him should he sniff it, chew it, inspect it, etc. This probably seems obvious since, while you are primarily concerned with your pup's safety, at the same time you do not want your belongings to be ruined. Breakables should be placed out of reach if your dog is to have full run of the house. If he is to be limited to certain places within the house, keep any potentially dangerous items in the "off-limits" areas. An electrical cord can pose a danger should the puppy decide to taste it—and who is going to convince a pup that it would not make a great chew toy? Cords should be fastened tightly against the wall. If your dog is going to spend time in a crate, make sure that there is nothing near his crate that he can reach if he sticks his curious little nose or paws through the openings. And just as you would with a child, keep all household cleaners and chemicals where the pup cannot get to them.

Be sure that you have removed all potentially poisonous vegetation from your yard. Nothing will deter your curious pup from sampling and playing in everything he can find.

It is just as important to make sure that the outside of your home is safe. Of course your puppy should never be unsupervised, but a pup let loose in the yard will want to run and explore, and he should be granted that freedom. Do not let a fence give you a false sense of security; you would be

surprised how crafty (and persistent) a dog can be in figuring out how to dig under and squeeze his way through small holes, or to jump or climb over a fence. The remedy is to make the fence high enough so that it really is impossible for your dog to get over it (6 feet should suffice), and well embedded into the ground. Be sure to repair or secure any gaps in the fence. Check the fence periodically to ensure that it is in good shape and make repairs as needed; a very determined pup may return to the same spot to "work on it" until he is able to get through.

POISONOUS PLANTS

Below is a partial list of plants that are considered poisonous. These plants can cause skin irritation, illness and even death. You should be aware of the types of plants that grow in your yard and that you keep in your home. Special care should be taken to rid your garden of dangerous plants and to keep all plants in the household out of your German Shepherd's reach.

American Blue Flag
Bachelor's Button
Barberry
Bog Iris
Boxwood
Buttercup
Cherry Pits
Chinese Arbor
Chokecherry
Christmas Rose
Climbing Lily
Crown of Thorns
Elderberry (berries)
Elephant Ear
English Ivy
False Acacia
Fern
Foxglove
Hellebore
Herb of Grace
Holly
Horse Chestnut
Iris (bulb)

Japanese Yew
Jerusalem Cherry
Jimson Weed
Lenten Rose
Lily of the Valley
Marigold
Milkwort
Mistletoe (berries)
Monkshood
Mullein
Narcissus
Peony
Persian Ivy
Rhododendron
Rhubarb
Shallon
Siberian Iris
Solomon's Seal
Star of Bethlehem
Water Lily
Wood Spurge
Wisteria
Yew

This young Shepherd gets along well with the family's two Tibetan Spaniels. If properly introduced, your Shepherd can be quite gregarious with all members of the household.

FIRST TRIP TO THE VET

So, you have picked out your puppy, your home and family are ready, now all you have to do is pick your German Shepherd up from the breeder and the fun begins, right? Well…not so fast. Something else you need to prepare for is your pup's first trip to the veterinarian. Perhaps the breeder can recommend someone in the area who specializes in German Shepherds, or maybe you know some other German Shepherd owners who can suggest a good vet. Either way, you should have an appointment arranged for your pup before you pick him up; plan on taking him for a checkup within the first few days of bringing him home.

The pup's first visit will consist of an overall examination to make sure that the pup does not have any problems that are not apparent to you. The veterinarian will also set up a schedule for the pup's vaccinations; the breeder will inform you of which ones the pup has already received and the vet can continue his vaccination schedule from there.

INTRODUCTION TO THE FAMILY

Everyone in the house will be excited about the puppy's coming home and will want to pet him and play with him, but it is best to keep the introductions low-key so as not to overwhelm the puppy. He is apprehensive already; it is the first time he has been separated from his mother and the breeder, and the ride to your home is likely the first time he has been in a car. The last thing

PET INSURANCE

Just like you can insure your car, your house and your own health, you likewise can insure your dog's health. Investigate a pet insurance policy by talking to your vet. Depending on the age of your dog, the breed and the kind of coverage you desire, your policy can be very affordable. Most policies cover accidental injuries, poisoning, and thousands of medical problems and illnesses, including cancers. Some carriers also offer routine care and immunization coverage, including heartworm preventative, prescription flea control, annual checkups, teeth cleaning, spaying/neutering, health screening and more. These policies are more costly than the others, but may be well worth the investment.

you want to do is smother him, as this will only frighten him further. This is not to say that human contact is not extremely necessary at this stage, because this is the time when an instant connection between the pup and his human family is formed. Gentle petting and soothing words should help console him, as well as just putting him down and letting him explore on his own (under your watchful eye, of course).

The pup may approach the family members or may busy himself with exploring for awhile. Gradually, each person should spend some time with the pup, one at a time, crouching down to get as close to the pup's level as possible and letting him sniff their hands and petting him gently. He definitely needs human attention and he needs to be touched—this is how to form an immediate bond. Just remember that the pup is experiencing a lot of things for the first time, all at the same time. There are new people, new noises, new smells and new things to investigate, so be gentle, be affectionate and be as comforting as you can be.

YOUR PUP'S FIRST NIGHT HOME

You have traveled home with your new charge safely in his crate. He's been to the vet for a thorough checkup; he's been weighed, his papers reviewed;

Curiosity is a way of life for all puppies. This pup seems ready to meet new friends and see the world.

perhaps he's even been vaccinated and wormed as well. He's met the family and licked the whole family, including the excited children and the less-than-happy cat. He's explored his area, his new bed, the yard and anywhere else he's been permitted. He's eaten his first meal at home and relieved himself in the proper place. He's heard lots of new sounds, smelled new friends and seen more of the outside world than ever before.

That was the just the first day! He's tuckered out and is ready for bed...or so you think!

It's puppy's first night and you are ready to say "Good night"— keep in mind that this is puppy's first night ever to be sleeping alone. His dam and littermates are no longer at paw's length and he's a bit scared, cold and lonely. Be reassuring to your new family

BETTER SOCIALIZATION
Thorough socialization includes not only meeting new people but also being introduced to new experiences such as riding in the car, having his coat brushed, hearing the television, walking in a crowd—the list is endless. The more your pup experiences, and the more positive the experiences are, the less of a shock and the less frightening it will be for your pup to encounter new things.

he will fall asleep without a peep. When the inevitable occurs, ignore the whining; he is fine. Be strong and keep his interest in mind. Do not allow your heart to become guilty and visit the pup. He will fall asleep.

Many breeders recommend placing a piece of bedding from his former home in his new bed so that he recognizes the scent of his littermates. Others still advise placing a hot water bottle in his bed for warmth. This latter may be a good idea provided the pup doesn't attempt to suckle—he'll get good and wet and may not fall asleep so fast.

Puppy's first night can be somewhat stressful for the pup and his new family. Remember that you are setting the tone of nighttime at your house. Unless you want to play with your pup every night at 10 p.m., midnight and 2 a.m., don't initiate the habit. Surely your family will thank you, and so will your pup!

PREVENTING PUPPY PROBLEMS

member, but this is not the time to spoil him and give in to his inevitable whining.

Puppies whine. They whine to let the others know where they are and hopefully to get company out of it. Place your pup in his new bed or crate in his room and close the crate door. Mercifully,

SOCIALIZATION
Now that you have done all of the preparatory work and have helped your pup get accustomed to his new home and family, it is about time for you to have some fun! Socializing your German Shepherd pup gives you the opportunity to show off your new

friend, and your pup gets to reap the benefits of being an adorable furry creature that people will coo over, want to pet and, in general, think is absolutely precious!

Besides getting to know his new family, your puppy should be exposed to other people, animals and situations. This will help him become better adjusted as he grows up and less prone to being timid or fearful of the new things he encounters. Your pup's socialization began at the breeder's, now it is your responsibility to continue. The socialization he receives up until the age of 12 weeks is the most critical, as this is the time when he forms his impressions of the outside world. Lack of socialization can manifest itself in fear and aggression as the dog grows up. He needs lots of human interaction, affection, handling and exposure to other animals. Be careful during the eight-to-ten-week-old period, also known as the fear period. The interaction he receives during this time should be gentle and reassuring.

Once your pup has received his necessary vaccinations, feel free to take him out and about (on his leash, of course). Take him around the neighborhood, take him on your daily errands, let people pet him, let him meet other dogs and pets, etc. Puppies do not have to try to make friends;

Play can be defined as supervised mischief! This playful pup may have a promising future in gardening.

there will be no shortage of people who will want to introduce themselves. Just make sure that you carefully supervise each interaction. If the neighborhood children want to say hello, for example, that is great—children and pups most often make great companions. But sometimes an excited child can unintentionally handle a pup too roughly, or an overzealous pup can playfully nip a little too hard. You want to make socialization experiences positive ones; what a pup learns during this very formative stage will impact his attitude toward future encounters. A pup that has a bad experience with a child may grow up to be a dog that is shy around or aggressive toward children, and you want your dog to be comfortable around everyone.

CONSISTENCY IN TRAINING

Dogs, being pack animals, naturally need a leader, or else they try to establish dominance in their packs. When you bring a dog into your family, who becomes the leader and who becomes the "pack" are entirely up to you! Your pup's intuitive quest for dominance, coupled with the fact that it is nearly impossible to look at an adorable German Shepherd pup, with his "puppy-dog" eyes and his too-big-for-his-head-still-floppy ears, and not cave in, give the pup almost an unfair advantage in getting the upper hand! And a pup will definitely test the waters to see what he can and cannot get away with. Do not give in to those pleading eyes—stand your ground when it comes to disciplining the pup and make sure that all family members do the same. It will only confuse the pup when Mother tells him to get off the couch when he is used to sitting up there with Father to watch the nightly news. Avoid discrepancies by having all

Do not allow your pup to chew on your shoes or pant leg. This will lead to problems later in life.

members of the household decide on the rules before the pup even comes home…and *be consistent* in enforcing them! Early training shapes the dog's personality, so you cannot be unclear in what you expect.

COMMON PUPPY PROBLEMS

The best way to prevent problems is to be proactive in stopping an undesirable behavior as soon as it starts. The old saying "You can't teach an old dog new tricks" does not necessarily hold true, but it is true that it is much easier to discourage bad behavior in a young developing pup than to wait until the pup's bad behavior becomes the adult dog's bad habit. There are some problems that are especially prevalent in puppies as they develop.

NIPPING

As puppies start to teethe, they feel the need to sink their teeth into anything…unfortunately that includes your fingers, arms, hair, toes…whatever happens to be available. You may find this behavior cute for about the first five seconds…until you feel just how sharp those puppy teeth are. This is something you want to discourage immediately and consistently with a firm "No!" (or whatever number of firm "Nos" it takes for him to understand that you mean business) and replace your finger with an appropriate chew toy. While this behavior is merely annoying when the dog is still young, it can become dangerous as your German Shepherd's adult teeth grow in and his jaws develop, if he thinks that it is okay to gnaw on human appendages. You do not want to take a chance with a German Shepherd, as this is a breed whose jaws become naturally very strong. He does not mean any harm with a friendly nip, but he also does not know his own strength.

CRYING/WHINING

Your pup will often cry, whine, whimper, howl or make some type of commotion when he is left alone. This is basically his way of calling out for attention, of calling out to make sure that you know he is there and that you have not forgotten about him. He feels insecure when he is left alone; for example, when you are out of the house and he is in his crate or when you are in another part of the house and he cannot see you. The noise he is making is an expression of the anxiety he feels at being alone, so he needs to be taught that being alone is okay. You are not actually training the dog to stop making noise, you are training him to feel comfortable when he is alone and thus removing the need for him to make the noise. This is where the cozy crate and toy come in handy. You want to know that he is safe when you are not there to supervise, and you know that he will be safe in his crate rather than roaming freely about the house. In order for the pup to stay in his crate without making a fuss, he needs to be comfortable in his crate. On that note, it is *extremely* important that the crate is *never* used as a form of punishment, or the pup will have a negative association with the crate.

Accustom the pup to the crate in short, gradually increasing time intervals in which you put him in the crate, maybe with a treat, and stay in the room with him. If he cries or makes a fuss, do not go to him, but stay in his sight. Gradually he will realize that staying in his crate is all right without your help, and it will not be so traumatic for him when you are not around. You may want to leave the radio on softly when you leave the house; the sound of human voices may be comforting to him.

PUPPY PROBLEMS

The majority of problems that are commonly seen in young pups will disappear as your dog gets older. However, how you deal with problems when he is young will determine how he reacts to discipline as an adult dog. It is important to establish who is boss (hopefully it will be you!) right away when you are first bonding with your dog. This bond will set the tone for the rest of your life together.

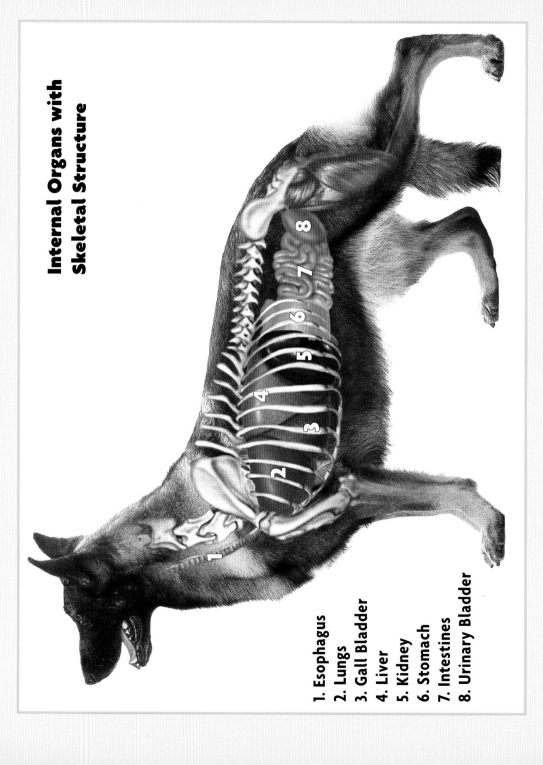

Internal Organs with Skeletal Structure

1. Esophagus
2. Lungs
3. Gall Bladder
4. Liver
5. Kidney
6. Stomach
7. Intestines
8. Urinary Bladder

EVERYDAY CARE OF YOUR
GERMAN SHEPHERD DOG

DIETARY AND FEEDING CONSIDERATIONS

You have probably heard it a thousand times: you are what you eat. Believe it or not, it's very true. For dogs, they are what you feed them because they have little choice in the matter. Even those people who truly want to feed their dogs the best often cannot do so because they do not know which foods are best for their dogs.

Dog foods are produced in three basic types: dry, semi-moist and canned. Dry foods are best for the cost-conscious because they are less expensive than semi-moist and canned. Dry foods contain the least fat and the most preservatives. Most canned foods are 60–70% water, while semi-moist foods are so full of sugar that they are the least preferred by owners, though dogs welcome them (as does a child candy).

Three stages of development must be considered when

FOOD PREFERENCE

Selecting the best dry dog food is difficult. There is no majority consensus among veterinary scientists as to the value of nutrient analyses (protein, fat, fiber, moisture, ash, cholesterol, minerals, etc.). All agree that feeding trials are what matter most, but you also have to consider the individual dog. The dog's weight, age and activity level, and what pleases his taste, all must be considered. It is probably best to take the advice of your veterinarian. Every dog's dietary requirements vary, even during the lifetime of a particular dog.

If your dog is fed a good dry food, it does not require supplements of meat or vegetables. Dogs do appreciate a little variety in their diets, so you may choose to stay with the same brand but vary the flavor. Alternatively, you may wish to add a little flavored stock to give a difference to the taste.

Your breeder will be a good source of advice on the best diet for a growing German Shepherd puppy.

selecting a diet for your dog: the puppy stage, the adult stage and the senior stage.

PUPPY DIETS

Puppies have a natural instinct to suck milk from their mother's teats. They should exhibit this behavior almost immediately. If they don't suckle within a few hours, the breeder should attempt to put them onto their mother's nipples. Their failure to feed means that the breeder has to feed them himself under the advice and guidance of a veterinarian. This will involve a baby bottle and a special formula. Their mother's milk is much better than any formula because it contains colostrum, a sort of antibiotic milk which protects the puppy during the first eight to ten weeks of their lives.

Puppies should be allowed to nurse for six weeks. The pups should be slowly weaned away from their mother by introducing small portions of canned food after they are about one month old.

By the time they are eight weeks old, they should be completely weaned and fed solely a puppy dry food. During this weaning period, their diet is most important as the puppy grows fastest during his first year of life. Growth foods can be recommended by your veterinarian and the puppy should be kept on this diet for up to 18 months.

Puppy diets should be balanced for your dog's needs and supplements of vitamins, minerals and protein should not be necessary.

ADULT DIETS

A dog is considered an adult when he has stopped growing. The growth is in height and/or length. Do not consider the dog's weight when the decision is made to switch from a puppy diet to a maintenance diet. Again you should rely upon your breeder or veterinarian to recommend an acceptable maintenance diet. Major dog-food manufacturers specialize in this type of food and it is important for you to select the one best suited to your dog's needs. Keep in mind that active dogs may have different requirements than sedate dogs.

A German Shepherd Dog reaches adulthood at about two years of age, though some dogs fully mature at 16 months, while others may take up to three years.

SENIOR DIETS

As dogs get older, their metabolism changes. The older dog usually exercises less, moves more slowly and sleeps more. This change in lifestyle and physiological performance requires a change in diet. Since these changes take place slowly, they might not be recognizable. What is easily recognizable is weight gain. By continually feeding your dog an adult-maintenance diet when it is slowing down metabolically, your dog will gain weight. Obesity in an older dog compounds the health problems that already accompany old age.

As your dog gets older, few of his organs function up to par. The kidneys slow down and the intestines become less efficient. These age-related factors are best handled with a change in diet and a change in feeding schedule to give smaller portions that are more easily digested.

There is no single best diet for every older dog. While many dogs do well on light or senior diets, other dogs do better on puppy diets or other special premium diets such as lamb and rice.

Be sensitive to your senior German Shepherd Dog's diet and this will help control other problems that may arise with your old friend.

Water should be available to your German Shepherd at all times. Offering water in a bowl stand and never allowing him to gulp water are excellent ways of warding off bloat.

WATER

Just as your dog needs proper nutrition from his food, water is an essential "nutrient" as well. Water keeps the dog's body properly hydrated and promotes normal function of the body's systems. During housebreaking, it is necessary to keep an eye on how much water your German

GRAIN-BASED DIETS

Some less expensive dog foods are based on grains and other plant proteins. While these products may appear to be attractively priced, many breeders prefer a diet based on animal proteins and believe that they are more conducive to your dog's health. Many grain-based diets rely on soy protein, which may cause flatulence (passing gas).

There are many cases, however, when your dog might require a special diet. These special requirements should only be recommended by your veterinarian.

A WORTHY INVESTMENT

Veterinary studies have proved that a high-quality diet pays off in your dog's coat quality, behavior and activity level. Invest in premium brands for the maximum payoff with your dog.

Shepherd is drinking, but once he is reliably trained he should have access to clean fresh water at all times. Make sure that the dog's water bowl is clean, and change the water often.

EXERCISE

All dogs require some form of exercise, regardless of breed. A sedentary lifestyle is as harmful to a dog as it is to a person. The German Shepherd happens to be an active breed that requires considerable exercise daily, but you don't have to be a weight-lifter or marathon runner to provide your dog with the exercise he needs. Regular walks, play sessions in the yard or letting the dog run free in a secure area under your supervision are all sufficient forms of exercise for the German Shepherd. For those who are more ambitious, you will find that your German Shepherd will be able to keep up with you on extra-long walks or the morning jog. Not only is exercise essential to keep the dog's body fit, it is essential to his mental well-being. A bored dog will find something to do, which often manifests itself in some type of destructive behavior. In this sense, it is essential for the owner's mental well-being as well!

The German Shepherd is an active breed that welcomes vigorous exercise and play with his owner. Shepherds love to feel a part of their owners' daily routines.

The hair of a German Shepherd Dog enlarged 1,200 times. Note the broken ends of the hair wall. This is the origin of dandruff.

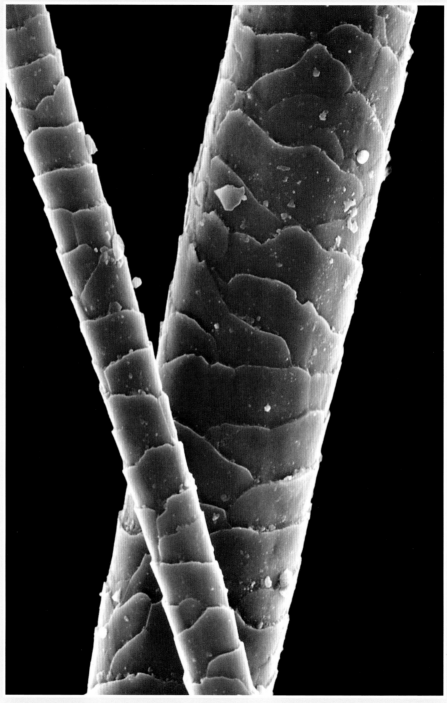

GROOMING

German Shepherds do not require fancy grooming or elaborate haircuts. Basically, the main goal in grooming the German Shepherd is to keep the dog's coat looking nice and maintained in good health. German Shepherds do shed, so during shedding seasons you will need to pay more attention to his coat. A metal rake or comb will aid in removing dead hair from the undercoat. A vigorous brushing will loosen much of the dead hair. Follow up with a metal comb to remove the hair that is being shed.

By making brushing a normal routine with your puppy, your German Shepherd Dog will grow to enjoy the experience.

GROOMING EQUIPMENT

How much grooming equipment you purchase will depend on how much grooming you are going to do. Here are some basics for the German Shepherd Dog:

- Natural bristle brush
- Slicker brush
- Metal comb
- Wide-tooth metal rake
- Scissors
- Rubber mat
- Dog shampoo
- Spray hose attachment
- Blow dryer
- Heavy towels
- Ear cleaner
- Cotton balls
- Nail clippers

BRUSHING

A natural bristle brush or a slicker brush can be used for regular routine brushing. Daily brushing is effective for removing dead hair and stimulating the dog's natural oils to add shine and a healthy look to the coat. The German Shepherd is not a breed that needs excessive grooming, but his heavy coat needs to be brushed daily as part of routine maintenance. Daily brushing will minimize tangles and mats, get rid of dust and dandruff and remove any dead hair. Regular grooming sessions are also a good way to spend time with your dog. Many dogs grow to like the feel of being brushed and will enjoy the daily routine.

BATHING

Dogs do not need to be bathed as often as humans, but occasional bathing is important for clean skin and a healthy, shiny coat.

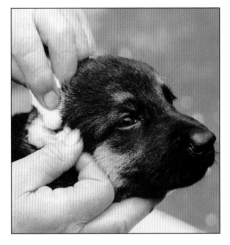

Again, like most anything, if you accustom your pup to being bathed as a puppy, it will be second nature by the time he grows up. You want your dog to be at ease in the bath or else it could end up a wet, soapy, messy ordeal for both of you!

Brush your German Shepherd thoroughly before wetting his coat. This will get rid of most mats and tangles, which are harder to remove when the coat is wet. Make that your dog has a good non-slip surface to stand on. Begin by wetting the dog's coat. A shower or hose attachment is necessary for thoroughly wetting and rinsing the coat. Check the water temperature to make sure that it is neither too hot nor too cold for the dog.

Next, apply shampoo to the dog's coat and work it into a good lather. You should purchase a shampoo that is made for dogs; do not use a product made for human hair. Wash the head last; you do not want shampoo to drip into the dog's eyes while you are washing the rest of his body. Work the shampoo all the way down to the skin. You can use this opportunity to check the skin for any bumps, bites or other abnormalities. Do not neglect any area of the body—get all of the hard-to-reach places.

Once the dog has been thoroughly shampooed, he requires an equally thorough rinsing. Shampoo left in the coat can be irritating and drying to the skin. Protect his eyes from the shampoo by shielding them with your hand and directing the flow of water in the opposite direction. You should also avoid getting

BATHING BEAUTY

Once you are sure that the dog is thoroughly rinsed, squeeze the excess water out of his coat with your hand and dry him with a heavy towel. You may choose to use a blow dryer on the lowest setting on his coat or just let it dry naturally. In cold weather, never allow your dog outside with a wet coat.

There are "dry bath" products on the market, which are sprays and powders intended for spot cleaning, that can be used between regular baths if necessary. They are not substitutes for regular baths, but they are easy to use for touch-ups as they do not require rinsing.

water in the ear canal. Be prepared for your dog to shake out his coat—you might want to stand back, but make sure you have a hold on the dog to keep him from running through the house.

EAR CLEANING

The ears should be kept clean and any excess hair inside the ear should be trimmed. Ears can be cleaned with a cotton ball and special cleaner or ear powder made especially for dogs. Be on the lookout for any signs of infection or ear-mite infestation. If your German Shepherd has been shaking his head or scratching at his ears frequently, this usually indicates a problem. If his ears have an unusual odor, this is a sure sign of mite infestation or infection, and a signal to have his ears checked by the veterinarian.

NAIL CLIPPING

Your German Shepherd should be accustomed to having his nails trimmed at an early age, since it will be part of your maintenance routine throughout his life. Not only does it look nicer, but a dog with long nails can cause injury if he jumps up or if he scratches someone unintentionally. Also, a long nail has a better chance of ripping and bleeding, or causing the feet to spread. A good rule of thumb is that if you can hear your dog's nails' clicking on the

PEDICURE TIP
A dog that spends a lot of time outside on a hard surface, such as cement or pavement, will have his nails naturally worn down and may not need to have them trimmed as often, except maybe in the colder months when he is not outside as much. Regardless, it is best to get your dog accustomed to the nail-trimming procedure at an early age so that he is used to it. Some dogs are especially sensitive about having their feet touched, but if a dog has experienced it since puppyhood, it should not bother him.

floor when he walks, his nails are too long.

Before you start cutting, make sure you can identify the "quick" in each nail. The quick is a blood vessel that runs through the center of each nail and grows rather close to the end. It will bleed if accidentally cut, which will be quite painful for the dog as it contains nerve endings. Keep some type of clotting agent on hand, such as a styptic pencil or styptic powder (the type used for shaving). This will stop the bleeding quickly when applied to the end of the cut nail. Do not panic if this happens, just stop the bleeding and talk soothingly to your dog. Once he has calmed down, move on to the next nail. It is better to clip a little at a time, particularly with dark-nailed dogs like the German Shepherd.

Hold your pup steady as you begin trimming his nails; you do not want him to make any sudden movements or run away. Talk to him soothingly and stroke his fur as you clip. Holding his foot in your hand, simply take off the end of each nail in one quick clip. You can purchase nail clippers that are specially made for dogs; you can probably find them wherever you buy pet or grooming supplies.

TRAVELING WITH YOUR DOG

CAR TRAVEL

You should accustom your German Shepherd to riding in a car at an early age. You may or may not often take him in the car, but at the very least he will need to go to the vet and you do not want these trips to be traumatic for the dog or problematic for you. The safest way for a dog to ride in the car is in his crate. If he uses a fiberglass crate in the house, you can use the same crate for travel. Wire crates can be used for travel, but fiberglass crates are safer.

Put the pup in the crate and see how he reacts. If he seems uneasy, you can have a passenger hold him on his lap while you drive. Another option is a specially made safety harness for dogs, which straps the dog in much like a seat belt. Do not let the dog roam loose in the vehicle—this is *very* dangerous! If you should stop

Offer your German Shepherd water when traveling. Be sure to stop often to let him relieve himself.

short, your dog can be thrown and injured. If the dog starts climbing on you and pestering you while you are driving, you will not be able to concentrate on the road. It is an unsafe situation for everyone—human and canine.

For long trips, be prepared to stop to let the dog relieve himself. Bring along whatever you need to clean up after him. You should bring along some paper towels in case he should have a potty accident in the car or become carsick.

AIR TRAVEL

Contact your chosen airline before proceeding with your travel plans that include your German Shepherd. The dog will be required to travel in a fiberglass crate and you should always check in advance with the airline regarding specific requirements for the crate's size, type and labeling. To help put the dog at ease, give him one of his favorite toys in the crate. Do not feed the dog for several hours prior to checking in so that you

NO PARKING

Never leave your dog alone in the car. In hot weather, your dog can die from the high temperature inside a closed vehicle; even a car parked in the shade can heat up very quickly. Leaving the window open is dangerous as well since the dog can hurt himself trying to get out.

minimize his need to relieve himself. However, some airlines require that the dog must be fed within a certain time frame before arriving at the airport, in which case a light meal is best. For long trips, you will have to attach food and water bowls to the dog's crate so that airline employees can tend to him between legs of the trip.

Make sure your dog is properly identified and that your contact information appears on his ID tags and on his crate. Your

Two dogs? Two crates. Dogs should not be allowed to roam freely in your vehicle.

Most German Shepherds love car trips, but you may find that you can't always take your dog along on vacations. You should find a suitable kennel in a convenient location so that your dog is in good hands when you travel.

German Shepherd will travel in a different area of the plane than the human passengers, so every rule must be strictly followed to prevent the risk of getting separated from your dog.

BOARDING

So you want to take a family vacation—and you want to include *all* members of the family. You would probably make arrangements for accommodations ahead of time anyway, but this is especially important when traveling with a dog. You do not want to make an overnight stop at the only place around for miles to find out that they do not allow dogs. Also, you do not want to reserve a room for your family without mentioning that you are bringing a dog, because, if it is against their policy, you may not have a place to stay.

Alternatively, if you are traveling and choose not to bring your German Shepherd, you will

COLLAR REQUIRED

If your dog gets lost, he is not able to ask for directions home. Identification tags fastened to the collar give important information—the dog's name, the owner's name, the owner's address and a telephone number where the owner can be reached. This makes it easy for whoever finds the dog to contact the owner and arrange to have the dog returned. An added advantage is that a person will be more likely to approach a lost dog who has ID tags on his collar; it tells the person that this is somebody's pet rather than a stray. This is the easiest and fastest method of identification, provided that the tags stay on the collar and the collar stays on the dog.

have to make arrangements for him while you are away. Some options are to bring him to a neighbor's house to stay while you are gone, to have a trusted neighbor stop by often or stay at your house or to bring your dog to a reputable boarding kennel. If you choose to board him at a kennel, you should stop by to see the facility and where the dogs are kept to make sure that it is clean. Talk to some of the employees and see how they treat the dogs—do they spend time with the dogs, play with them, exercise them, etc.? You know that your German Shepherd will not be happy unless he gets regular activity. Also find out the kennel's policy on vaccinations and what they require. This is for all of the dogs' safety, since when dogs are kept together, there is a greater risk of diseases being passed from dog

Your German Shepherd Dog should have a sturdy collar with his identification tags and licenses attached.

to dog. Many veterinarians offer boarding facilities; this is another good option.

IDENTIFICATION

Your German Shepherd is your valued companion and friend. That is why you always keep a close eye on him and you have made sure that he cannot escape from the yard or wriggle out of his collar and run away from you. However, accidents can happen and there may come a time when your dog unexpectedly gets separated from you. If this unfortunate event should occur, the first thing on your mind will be finding him. Proper identification, including ID tags and possibly a tattoo or microchip, will increase the chances of his being returned to you safely and quickly.

GOING ABROAD

For international travel, you will have to make arrangements well in advance (perhaps months), as countries' regulations pertaining to bringing in animals differ. There may be special health certificates and/or vaccinations that your dog will need before taking the trip; sometimes this has to be done within a certain time frame. When traveling to rabies-free countries, you will need to bring proof of the dog's rabies vaccination and there will likely be a quarantine period upon arrival.

With dedication and training, your German Shepherd will be jumping through hoops in no time!

TRAINING YOUR
GERMAN SHEPHERD DOG

Living with an untrained dog is a lot like owning a piano that you do not know how to play—it is a nice object to look at, but it does not do much more than that to bring you pleasure. Now try taking piano lessons, and suddenly the piano comes alive and brings forth magical sounds and rhythms that set your heart singing and your body swaying.

The same is true with your German Shepherd. At first you enjoy seeing him around the house. He does not do much with you other than to need food, water and exercise. Come to think of it, he does not bring you much joy, either. He is a big responsibility with a very small return. And often, he develops unacceptable behaviors that annoy you, to say nothing of bad habits that may end up costing you great sums of money. This is not a good thing!

Now train your German Shepherd. Enroll in an obedience class. Teach him good manners as you learn how and why he behaves the way he does. Find out how to communicate with your dog and how to recognize and understand his communications with you. Suddenly the dog takes on a new role in your life—he is smart, interesting, well behaved and fun to be with, and he demonstrates his bond of devotion to you daily. In other words, your German Shepherd does wonders for your ego because he constantly reminds you that you are not only his leader, you are his hero! Miraculous things have happened—you have a wonderful

Training is necessary to ensure that your German Shepherd Dog grows up to be polite and well behaved.

dog (even your family and friends have noticed the transformation!) and you feel good about yourself.

Those involved with teaching dog obedience and counseling owners about their dogs' behavior have discovered some interesting facts about dog ownership. For example, training dogs when they are puppies results in the highest rate of success in developing well-mannered and well-adjusted adult dogs. Training an older dog, say from six months to six years of age, can produce almost equal results, providing that the owner accepts the dog's slower rate of learning capability and is willing to work patiently to help the dog succeed at developing to his fullest potential. Unfortunately, the patience factor is what many owners of untrained adult dogs

lack, so they do not persist until their dogs are successful at learning particular behaviors.

Training a puppy, for example, aged 8 to 16 weeks (20 weeks at the most), is like working with a dry sponge in a pool of water. The pup soaks up whatever you show him and constantly looks for more things to do and learn. At this early age, his body is not yet producing hormones, and therein lies the reason for such a high rate of success. Without hormones, he is focused on his owners and not particularly interested in investigating other places, dogs, people, etc. You are his leader: his provider of food, water, shelter and security. Therefore, he latches onto you and wants to stay close. He will usually follow you from room to room, will not let you

This German Shepherd pup knows how to cool off!

More than one dog means more patience and effort in training. Each dog needs a proper education in order to achieve a peaceful multi-pet home.

out of his sight when you are outdoors with him and will respond in like manner to the people and animals you encounter. If, for example, you greet a friend warmly, he will be happy to greet the person as well. If, however, you are hesitant, even anxious, about the approach of a stranger, he will respond to the person accordingly.

Once the puppy begins to produce hormones, his natural curiosity emerges and he begins to investigate the world around him. It is at that time when you may notice that the untrained dog begins to wander away from you and even ignore your commands to stay close. When this behavior becomes a problem, the owner has two choices: get rid of the dog or train him. It is

strongly urged that you choose the latter option.

Occasionally there are no classes available within a reasonable distance from the owner's home. Sometimes there are classes available but the tuition is too costly. Whatever the circumstances, the solution to the problem of training your German Shepherd without formal

FAMILY TIES
If you have other pets in the home and/or interact often with the pets of friends and other family members, your pup will respond to those pets in much the same manner as you do. It is only when you show fear of or resentment toward another animal that he will act fearful or unfriendly.

Your puppy is just waiting to learn and soak up whatever you teach him—take the opportunity to mold him into a polite canine citizen.

obedience classes lies within the pages of this book.

This chapter is devoted to helping you train your German Shepherd at home. If the recommended procedures are followed faithfully, you may expect positive results that will prove rewarding to both you and your dog.

Whether your German Shepherd is a puppy or a mature adult, the methods of teaching and the techniques we use in training basic behaviors are the

German Shepherds are eager and alert, traits evident from puppyhood.

same. After all, no dog, whether puppy or adult, likes harsh or inhumane methods. All creatures, however, respond favorably to gentle motivational methods and sincere praise and encouragement. Now let us get started.

OBEDIENCE SCHOOL

A basic obedience beginner's class usually lasts for six to eight weeks. Dog and owner attend an hour-long lesson once a week and practice for a few minutes, several times a day, each day at home. If done properly, the whole procedure will result in a well-mannered dog and an owner who delights in living with a pet that is eager to please and enjoys doing things with his owner.

Canine Development Schedule

It is important to understand how and at what age a puppy develops into adulthood. If you are a puppy owner, consult the following Canine Development Schedule to determine the stage of development your German Shepherd puppy is currently experiencing. This knowledge will help you as you work with the puppy in the weeks and months ahead.

Period	Age	Characteristics
FIRST TO THIRD	BIRTH TO SEVEN WEEKS	Puppy needs food, sleep and warmth, and responds to simple and gentle touching. Needs mother for security and disciplining. Needs littermates for learning and interacting with other dogs. Pup learns to function within a pack and learns pack order of dominance. Begin socializing pup with adults and children for short periods. Pup begins to become aware of his environment.
FOURTH	EIGHT TO TWELVE WEEKS	Brain is fully developed. Needs socializing with outside world. Remove from mother and littermates. Needs to change from canine pack to human pack. Human dominance necessary. Fear period occurs between 8 and 16 weeks. Avoid fright and pain.
FIFTH	THIRTEEN TO SIXTEEN WEEKS	Training and formal obedience should begin. Less association with other dogs, more with people, places, situations. Period will pass easily if you remember this is pup's change-to-adolescence time. Be firm and fair. Flight instinct prominent. Permissiveness and over-disciplining can do permanent damage. Praise for good behavior.
JUVENILE	FOUR TO EIGHT MONTHS	Another fear period about 7 to 8 months of age. It passes quickly, but be cautious of fright and pain. Sexual maturity reached. Dominant traits established. Dog should understand sit, down, come and stay by now.

NOTE: THESE ARE APPROXIMATE TIME FRAMES. ALLOW FOR INDIVIDUAL DIFFERENCES IN PUPPIES.

HOUSEBREAKING

Your German Shepherd puppy will find a favorite spot in which to relieve himself. Be sure that spot is convenient for you so that you can take him there when necessary.

You can train a puppy to relieve himself wherever you choose. For example, city dwellers often train their puppies to relieve themselves during walks because large plots of grass are not readily available. Of course, these people must be prepared to clean up public deposits. Sub-urbanites, on the other hand, usually have yards to accommodate their dogs' needs.

Outdoor training includes such surfaces as grass, dirt and cement. Indoor training usually means training your dog to newspaper, although this is not a good option with a large dog like the German Shepherd.

When deciding on the surface and location that you will want your German Shepherd to use, be sure it is going to be permanent. Training your dog to grass and then changing your mind two months later is extremely difficult for both dog and owner.

Next, choose the command you will use each and every time you want your puppy to void. "Go hurry up" and "Go make" are examples of commands commonly used by dog owners.

Get in the habit of asking the puppy, "Do you want to go hurry up?" (or whatever your chosen relief command is) before you take him out. That way, when he becomes an adult, you will be able to determine if he wants to go out when you ask him. A confirmation will be signs of interest like wagging his tail, watching you intently, going to the door, etc.

PUPPY'S NEEDS

The puppy needs to relieve himself after play periods, after each meal, after he has been sleeping and any time he indicates that he is looking for a place to urinate or defecate. The urinary and intestinal tract muscles of very young puppies are not fully developed. Therefore, like human babies, puppies need to relieve themselves frequently.

Take your puppy out often—every hour for an eight-week-old, for example. The older the puppy, the less often he will need to relieve himself. Finally, as a mature healthy adult, he will require only three to five relief trips per day.

HOUSING

Since the types of housing and control you provide for your puppy have a direct relationship on the success of house-training, we consider the various aspects of both before we begin training.

Bringing a new puppy home and turning him loose in your house can be compared to turning a child loose in a sports arena and telling the child that the place is all his! The sheer enormity of the place would be too much for him to handle.

Instead, offer the puppy clearly defined areas where he can play, sleep, eat and live. A room of the house where the family gathers is the most obvious choice. Puppies are social animals and need to feel a part of the pack right from the start. Hearing your voice, watching you while you are doing things and smelling you nearby are all positive reinforcers that he is now a member of your pack. Usually a family room, the kitchen or a nearby adjoining breakfast nook is ideal for providing safety and security for both puppy and owner.

Within that room there should be a smaller area that the puppy can call his own. A cubbyhole, a wire or fiberglass dog crate or a partitioned (not boarded!) corner from which he can view the activities of his new family will be fine. The size of the area or crate is the key

CONSISTENCY PAYS OFF

Dogs need consistency in their feeding schedule, exercise and relief visits, and in the verbal commands you use. If you use "Stay" on Monday and "Stay here, please" on Tuesday, you will confuse your dog. Don't demand perfect behavior during training sessions and then let him have the run of the house the rest of the day. Above all, lavish praise on your pet consistently every time he does something right. The more he feels he is pleasing you, the more willing he will be to learn.

factor here. The area must be large enough for the puppy to lay down and stretch out as well as stand up without rubbing his head on the top, yet small enough so that he cannot relieve himself at one end and sleep at the other without coming into contact with his droppings.

Dogs are, by nature, clean animals and will not remain close to their relief areas unless forced to do so. In those cases, they then become dirty dogs and usually remain that way for life.

The crate or area should be lined with a clean towel and offer one toy, no more. Do not put food or water in the crate, as eating and drinking will activate his digestive processes and ultimately defeat your purpose as well as make the puppy very uncomfortable as he attempts to "hold it."

THE CLEAN LIFE
By providing sleeping and resting quarters that fit the dog, and offering frequent opportunities to relieve himself outside his quarters, the puppy quickly learns that the outdoors, and particularly his chosen relief site, is the place to go when he needs to urinate or defecate. It also reinforces his innate desire to keep his sleeping quarters clean. This, in turn, helps develop the muscle control that will eventually produce a dog with clean living habits.

Recognize the signs—this German Shepherd Dog is ready to go out! Some dogs always seem to be on the wrong side of the door.

CONTROL

By *control*, we mean helping the puppy to create a lifestyle pattern that will be compatible to that of his human pack (*you!*). Just as we guide little children to learn our way of life, we must show the puppy when it is time to play, eat, sleep, exercise and even entertain himself.

Your puppy should always sleep in his crate. He should also learn that, during times of household confusion and excessive human activity such as at breakfast when family members are preparing for the day, he can play by himself in relative safety and comfort in his crate. Each time you leave the puppy alone, he should be crated. Puppies are chewers. They cannot tell the difference between lamp cords, television wires, shoes, table legs, etc. Chewing into a television wire, for example, can be fatal to the puppy, while a shorted wire can start a fire in the house.

If the puppy chews on the arm of the chair when he is alone, you will probably discipline him angrily when you get home. Thus, he makes the association that your coming home means he is going to be punished. (He will not remember chewing the chair and is incapable of making the association of the discipline with his naughty deed.)

Times of excitement, such as family parties, visits from friends, etc., can be fun for the puppy, providing he can view the activities from the security of his crate. He is not underfoot and he is not being fed all sorts of tidbits that will probably cause him stomach distress, yet he still feels a part of the fun.

SCHEDULE

A puppy should be taken to his relief area each time he is released from his crate, after meals, after play sessions, when he first awakens in the morning (at age eight weeks, this can mean 5 a.m.!) and whenever he indicates by circling or sniffing busily that he needs to urinate or defecate. For a puppy less than ten weeks of age, a routine of taking him out every hour is necessary. As the puppy grows, he will be able to wait for longer periods of time.

Keep trips to his relief area short. Stay no more than five or six minutes and then return to the house. If he goes during that time, praise him lavishly and take him indoors immediately. If he does not, but he has an accident when you go back indoors, pick him up immediately, say "No! No!" and return to his relief area. Wait a few minutes, then return to the house again. *Never* hit a puppy or put his face in urine or excrement when he has an accident!

Once indoors, put the puppy in his crate until you have had time to clean up his accident. Then release him to the family area and watch him more closely than before. Chances are, his accident was a result of your not picking up his signal or waiting too long before offering him the opportunity to relieve himself.

PAPER CAPER

Never line your pup's sleeping area with newspaper. Puppy litters are usually raised on newspaper and, once in your home, the puppy will immediately associate newspaper with voiding. Never put newspaper on any floor while house-training, as this will only confuse the puppy. If you are paper-training him, use paper in his designated relief area only. Finally, restrict water intake after evening meals. Offer a few licks at a time—never let a young puppy gulp water after meals.

Never hold a grudge against the puppy for accidents.

Let the puppy learn that going outdoors means it is time to relieve himself, not play. Once trained, he will be able to play indoors and out and still differentiate between the times for play versus the times for relief.

Help him develop regular hours for naps, being alone, playing by himself and just resting, all in his crate. Encourage him to entertain himself while you are busy with your activities. Let him learn that having you near is comforting, but it is not your main purpose in life to provide him with undivided attention.

Each time you put your puppy in his crate, tell him "Crate time!" (or whatever command you

THE SUCCESS METHOD

6 Steps to Successful Crate Training

1 Tell the puppy "Crate time!" and place him in the crate with a small treat (a piece of cheese or half of a biscuit). Let him stay in the crate for five minutes while you are in the same room. Then release him and praise lavishly. Never release him when he is fussing. Wait until he is quiet before you let him out.

2 Repeat Step 1 several times a day.

3 The next day, place the puppy in the crate as before. Let him stay there for ten minutes. Do this several times.

4 Continue building time in five-minute increments until the puppy stays in his crate for 30 minutes with you in the room. Always take him to his relief area after prolonged periods in his crate.

5 Now go back to Step 1 and let the puppy stay in his crate for five minutes, this time while you are out of the room.

6 Once again, build crate time in five-minute increments with you out of the room. When the puppy will stay willingly in his crate (he may even fall asleep!) for 30 minutes with you out of the room, he will be ready to stay in it for several hours at a time.

choose). Soon, he will run to his crate when he hears you say those words.

In the beginning of his training, do not leave him in his crate for prolonged periods of time except during the night when everyone is sleeping. Make his experience with his crate a pleasant one and, as an adult, he will love his crate and willingly stay in it for several hours. There are millions of people who go to work every day and leave their adult dogs crated while they are away. The dogs accept this as their lifestyle and look forward to "crate time." Once your Shepherd is reliably housebroken, you can trust him in the home—and a guard dog protects his property better when he's not crated!

Crate training provides safety for you, the puppy and the home. It also provides the puppy with a feeling of security, and that helps the puppy achieve self-confidence and clean habits.

Crate training is wonderful. Your German Shepherd's crate should be large enough that he is comfortable in it, and can be used for safe confinement indoors and out.

Remember that one of the primary ingredients in house-training your puppy is control. Regardless of your lifestyle, there will always be occasions when you will need to have a place where your dog can stay and be happy and safe. Crate training is the answer for now and in the future.

In conclusion, a few key elements are really all you need for a successful crate-training

THE SUCCESS METHOD

Success that comes by luck is usually short-lived. Success that comes by well-thought-out proven methods is often more easily achieved and permanent. This is the Success Method. It is designed to give you, the puppy owner, a simple yet proven way to help your puppy develop clean living habits and a feeling of security in his new environment.

Once the housebreaking routine is learned, it is a ritual that your dog will follow throughout his life.

method—consistency, frequency, praise, control and supervision. By following these procedures with a normal, healthy puppy, you and the puppy will soon be past the stage of accidents and ready to move on to a clean and rewarding life together.

PRACTICE MAKES PERFECT!

- Have training lessons with your dog every day in several short segments—three to five times a day for a few minutes at a time is ideal.
- Do not have long practice sessions. The dog will become easily bored.
- Never practice when you are tired, ill, worried or in an otherwise negative mood. This will transmit to the dog and may have an adverse effect on his performance.

   Think fun, short and above all positive! End each session on a high note, rather than a failed exercise, and make sure to give a lot of praise. Enjoy the training and help your dog enjoy it, too.

ROLES OF DISCIPLINE, REWARD AND PUNISHMENT

Discipline, training one to act in accordance with rules, brings order to life. It is as simple as that. Without discipline, particularly in a group society, chaos reigns supreme and the group will eventually perish. Humans and canines are social animals and need some form of discipline in order to function effectively. They must procure food, reproduce to keep the species going and protect their home base and their young.

   If there were no discipline in the lives of social animals, they would eventually die from starvation and/or predation by other stronger animals. In the case of domestic canines, dogs need discipline in their lives in order to understand how their pack (you and other family members) functions and how they must act in order to survive.

   A large humane society in a highly populated area recently surveyed dog owners regarding their satisfaction with their relationships with their dogs. People who had trained their dogs were 75% more satisfied with their pets than those who had never trained their dogs.

   Dr. Edward Thorndike, a noted psychologist, established *Thorndike's Theory of Learning*, which states that a behavior that results in a pleasant event tends to be repeated. Likewise, a behavior that results in an unpleasant event tends not to be repeated. It is this theory on which most training methods are based today. For example, if you manipulate a dog to perform a specific behavior and reward him for doing it, he is likely to do it again because he enjoyed the end result.

Occasionally, punishment, a penalty inflicted for an offense, is necessary. The best type of punishment often comes from an outside source. For example, a child is told not to touch the stove because he may get burned. He disobeys and touches the stove. In doing so, he receives a burn. From that time on, he respects the heat of the stove and avoids contact with it. Therefore, a behavior that results in an unpleasant event tends not to be repeated.

A good example of a dog learning the hard way is the dog who chases the house cat. He is told many times to leave the cat alone, yet he persists in teasing the cat. Then, one day he begins chasing the cat but the cat turns and swipes a claw across the dog's face, leaving him with a painful gash on his nose. The final result is that the dog stops chasing the cat.

TRAINING EQUIPMENT

COLLAR

A simple buckle collar is fine for most dogs, constructed of nylon (for a pup) and of leather (for an adult). One who pulls mightily on the leash may require a choke collar for training. Always be certain that the collar fits snugly but not too tightly. A puppy Shepherd's neck (and the fur around it) grows every day, so keep a close eye on his collar.

LEASH

A 6-foot leash is recommended, preferably made of leather or nylon. The leash you choose should be one with which you are able to work easily, comfortable for both the dog and you and perfectly safe.

TREATS

Have a bag of treats on hand. Something nutritious and easy to swallow works best; use a soft treat, a chunk of cheese or a piece

PLAN TO PLAY

The puppy should also have regular play and exercise sessions when he is with you or a family member. Exercise for a very young puppy can consist of a short walk around the house or yard. Playing can include fetching games with a large ball or a special toy. (All puppies teethe and need soft things upon which to chew.) Remember to restrict play periods to indoors within his living area (the family room, for example) until he is completely house-trained.

Working and service dogs wear special harnesses when performing their duties. These leather harnesses are worn by German Shepherds that work as guide dogs.

Seeing Eye® dogs undergo lengthy specialized training to reliably perform as guide dogs.

of cooked chicken rather than a dry biscuit. By the time the dog gets done chewing a dry treat, he will forget why he is being rewarded in the first place! By the way, using food rewards will not teach a dog to beg at the table—the only way to teach a dog to beg at the table is to give him food from the table. In training, rewarding the dog with a food treat away from the table will help him associate praise and the treats with learning new behaviors that obviously please his owner.

TRAINING BEGINS: ASK THE DOG A QUESTION

In order to teach your dog anything, you must first get his attention. After all, he cannot learn anything if he is looking away from you with his mind on something else.

To get his attention, ask him "School?" and immediately walk over to him and give him a treat as you tell him "Good dog." Wait a minute or two and repeat the

routine, this time with a treat in your hand as you approach the dog to within a foot of him. Do not go directly to him, but stop about a foot short of him and hold out the treat as you ask "School?" He will see you approaching with a treat in your hand and most likely begin walking toward you. As you meet, give him the treat and praise again.

The third time, ask the question, have a treat in your hand and walk only a short distance toward the dog so that he must walk almost all the way to you. As he reaches you, give him the treat and praise again.

By this time, the dog will probably be getting the idea that if he pays attention to you, especially when you ask that question, it will pay off in treats and fun activities for him. In other words, he learns that "school" means doing fun things with you that result in treats and positive attention for him.

Remember that the dog does not understand your verbal language, he only recognizes sounds. Your question translates to a series of sounds for him, and those sounds become the signal to go to you and pay attention; if he does, he will get to interact with you plus receive treats and praise.

THE BASIC COMMANDS

TEACHING SIT

Now that you have the dog's attention, hold the leash in your left hand and the food treat in your right. Place your food hand at the dog's nose and let him lick the treat but not take it from you. Say "Sit" and slowly raise your food hand from in front of the dog's nose up over his head so that he is looking at the ceiling. As he bends his head upward, he will have to bend his knees to maintain his balance. As he bends his knees, he will assume a sit position. At that point, release the food treat and praise lavishly with comments such as "Good dog! Good sit!," etc. Remember to always praise enthusiastically, because dogs relish verbal praise from their owners and feel so proud of themselves whenever they accomplish a behavior.

You will not use food forever in getting the dog to obey your commands. Food is only used to teach new behaviors, and once the dog knows what you want when you give a specific command, you will wean him off the food treats but still maintain the verbal praise. After all, you will always have your voice with you, but there will be many times when you have no food rewards yet you expect the dog to obey.

Sit is one of the first commands you will teach your German Shepherd Dog.

Using a treat to coax your dog into the sit position is a proven method of teaching the exercise.

where they meet above the spinal cord. Do not push down on the dog's shoulders; simply rest your left hand there so you can guide the dog to lie down close to your left leg rather than to swing away from your side when he drops.

Now place the food hand at the dog's nose, say "Down" very softly (almost a whisper) and slowly lower the food hand to the dog's front feet. When the food hand reaches the floor, begin moving it forward along the floor in front of the dog. Keep talking softly to the dog, saying things like, "Do you want this treat? You can do this, good dog." Your reassuring tone of voice will help calm the dog as he tries to follow the food hand in order to get the treat.

When the dog's elbows touch the floor, release the food and praise softly. Try to get the dog to maintain that down position for several seconds before you let him sit up again. The goal here is to

TEACHING DOWN

Teaching the down exercise is easy when you understand how the dog perceives the down position, and it is very difficult when you do not. In addition, teaching the down exercise using the wrong method can sometimes make the dog develop such a fear of the down that he either runs away when you say "Down" or he attempts to bite the person who tries to force him down.

Have the dog sit close alongside your left leg, facing in the same direction as you are. Hold the leash in your left hand and a food treat in your right. Now place your left hand lightly on the top of the dog's shoulders

LANGUAGE BARRIER

Dogs do not understand our language. They can be trained to react to a certain sound, at a certain volume. If you say "No, Oliver" in a very soft, pleasant voice, it will not have the same meaning as "No, Oliver!" when you shout it as loud as you can. You should never use the dog's name during a reprimand, just the command "No" so that he does not associate his name with being reprimanded.

get the dog to settle down and not feel threatened in the down position.

TEACHING STAY

It is easy to teach the dog to stay in either a sit or a down position. Again, we use food and praise during the teaching process as we help the dog to understand exactly what it is that we are expecting him to do.

To teach the sit/stay, start with the dog sitting on your left side as before and hold the leash in your left hand. Have a food treat in your right hand and place your food hand at the dog's nose. Say "Stay" and step out on your right foot to stand directly in front of the dog, toe to toe, as he licks and nibbles the treat. Be sure to keep his head facing upward to maintain the sit position. Count to five and then swing around to stand next to the dog again with him on your left. As soon as you get back to the original position, release the food and praise lavishly.

To teach the down/stay, do the down as previously described. As soon as the dog lies down, say "Stay" and step out on your right foot just as you did in the sit/stay. Count to five and then return to stand beside the dog with him on your left side. Release the treat and praise as always.

Within a week or ten days, you can begin to add a bit of distance between you and your dog when you leave him. When you do, use your left hand open with the palm facing the dog as a stay signal, much the same as the hand signal a police officer uses to stop traffic at an intersection. Hold the food treat in your right hand as before, but this time the food is not touching the dog's nose. He will watch the food hand and quickly learn that he is going to get that treat as soon as you return to his side.

When you can stand 1 yard away from your dog for 30 seconds, you can then begin building time and distance in both stays. Eventually, the dog can be expected to remain in the

DOUBLE JEOPARDY

A dog in jeopardy never lies down. He stays alert on his feet because instinct tells him that he may have to run away or fight for his survival. Therefore, if a dog feels threatened or anxious, he will not lie down. Consequently, it is important to keep the dog calm and relaxed as he learns the down exercise.

stay position for prolonged periods of time until you return to him or call him to you. Always praise lavishly when he stays.

TEACHING COME

If you make teaching "Come" a fun experience, you should never have a student that does not love the game or that fails to come when called. The secret, it seems, is never to teach the word "come."

At times when an owner most wants his dog to come when called, the owner is likely upset or anxious and he allows these feelings to come through in the tone of his voice when he calls his dog. Hearing that desperation in his owner's voice, the dog fears the results of going to him and therefore either

Practice is what makes the difference between temporary training and a permanent education. You must plan to practice your dog's mastered commands every day.

disobeys outright or runs in the opposite direction. The secret, therefore, is to teach the dog a game and, when you want him to come to you, simply play the game. It is practically a no-fail solution!

To begin, have several members of your family take a few food treats and each go into a different room in the house. Take turns calling the dog, and each person should celebrate the dog's finding him with a treat and lots of happy praise. When a person calls the dog, he is actually inviting the dog to find him and get a treat as a reward for "winning."

A few turns of the "Where are you?" game and the dog will figure out that everyone is playing the game and that each person has a big celebration awaiting his success at locating them. Once the dog learns to love the game, simply calling out "Where are you?" will bring him running from wherever he is when he hears that all-important question.

The come command is recognized as one of the most important things to teach a dog, so it is interesting to note that there are trainers who work with thousands of dogs and never teach the actual word "come." Yet these dogs will race to respond to a person who uses the dog's name followed by "Where

> ## "WHERE ARE YOU?"
> When calling the dog, do not say "Come." Say things like, "Rover, where are you? See if you can find me! I have a biscuit for you!" Keep up a constant line of chatter with coaxing sounds and frequent questions such as, "Where are you?" The dog will learn to follow the sound of your voice to locate you and receive his reward.

are you?" In one instance, for example, a woman has a 12-year-old companion dog who went blind, but who never fails to locate her owner when asked, "Where are you?"

Children particularly love to play this game with their dogs. Children can hide in smaller places like a shower stall or bathtub, behind a bed or under a table. The dog needs to work a little bit harder to find these hiding places, but, when he does, he loves to celebrate with a treat and a tussle with a favorite youngster.

TEACHING HEEL
Heeling means that the dog walks beside the owner without pulling. It takes time and patience on the owner's part to succeed at teaching the dog that he (the owner) will not proceed unless the dog is walking calmly beside him. Pulling out ahead on the leash is definitely not acceptable.

Begin with holding the leash in your left hand as the dog sits beside your left leg. Hold the loop end of the leash in your right hand but keep your left hand short on the leash so it keeps the dog close to you.

Say "Heel" and step forward on your left foot. Keep the dog close to you and take three steps. Stop and have the dog sit next to you in what we now call the heel position. Praise verbally, but do not touch the dog. Hesitate a moment and begin again with "Heel," taking three steps and stopping, at which point the dog is told to sit again.

Heel training will be appreciated every day when you walk your dog. A well-trained German Shepherd is a pleasure to walk and a joy to be around.

TUG OF WALK?

If you begin teaching the heel by taking long walks and letting the dog pull you along, he misinterprets this action as an acceptable form of taking a walk. When you pull back on the lead to counteract his pulling, he reads that tug as a signal to pull even harder!

Your goal here is to have the dog walk those three steps without pulling on the leash. When he will walk calmly beside you for three steps without pulling, increase the number of steps you take to five. When he will walk politely beside you while you take five steps, you can increase the length of your walk to ten steps. Keep increasing the length of your stroll until the dog will walk quietly beside you without pulling as long as you want him to heel. When you stop heeling, indicate to the dog that the exercise is over by verbally praising as you pet him and say "Okay, good dog." The "Okay" is used as a release word, meaning that the exercise is finished and the dog is free to relax.

If you are dealing with a dog who insists on pulling you around, simply "put on your brakes" and stand your ground until the dog realizes that the two of you are not going anywhere

German Shepherds have excelled in Schutzhund training for generations. If yours is to be a guard dog, you might consider sleeve work with a professional trainer.

until he is beside you and moving at your pace, not his. It may take some time just standing there to convince the dog that you are the leader and you will be the one to decide on the direction and speed of your travel.

Each time the dog looks up at you or slows down to give a slack leash between the two of you, quietly praise him and say, "Good heel. Good dog." Eventually, the dog will begin to respond and within a few days he will be walking politely beside you without pulling on the leash. At first, the training sessions should be kept short and very positive; soon the dog will be able to walk nicely with you for increasingly

A BORN PRODIGY
Occasionally, a dog and owner who have not attended formal classes have been able to earn entry-level titles by obtaining competition rules and regulations from a local kennel club and practicing on their own to a degree of perfection. Obtaining the higher level titles, however, almost always requires extensive training under the tutelage of experienced instructors. In addition, the more difficult levels require more specialized equipment whereas the lower levels do not.

longer distances. Remember also to give the dog free time and the opportunity to run and play when you are done with heel practice.

All work and no play... These well-trained police dogs demonstrate how obedient and intelligent the German Shepherd can be.

Your German Shepherd can be taught to retrieve upon command. You can even teach your dog to bring you the newspaper!

WEANING OFF FOOD IN TRAINING

Food is used in training new behaviors, yet once the dog understands what behavior goes with a specific command, it is time to start weaning him off the food treats. At first, give a treat after each exercise. Then, start to give a treat only after every other exercise. Mix up the times when you offer a food reward and the times when you only offer praise so that the dog will never know when he is going to receive both food and praise and when he is going to receive only praise. This is called a variable ratio reward

system and it proves successful because there is always the chance that the owner will produce a treat, so the dog never stops trying for that reward. No matter what, *always* give verbal praise.

OBEDIENCE CLASSES

As previously discussed, it is a good idea to enroll in an obedience class if one is available in your area. Many areas have dog clubs that offer basic obedience training as well as preparatory classes for obedience competition. There are also local dog trainers who offer similar classes. If you intend to show your German Shepherd, inquire about handling classes with a local dog club.

At obedience trials, dogs can earn titles at various levels of competition. The beginning levels of competition include basic behaviors such as sit, down, heel, etc. The more advanced levels of competition include jumping, retrieving, scent discrimination and signal work. The advanced levels require a dog and owner to put a lot of time and effort into their training; the titles that can be earned at these levels of competition are very prestigious.

OTHER ACTIVITIES FOR LIFE

Whether a dog is trained in the structured environment of a class or alone with his owner at home, there are many activities that can bring fun and rewards to both owner and dog once they have mastered basic control.

Teaching the dog to help out around the home, in the yard or on the farm provides great satisfaction to both dog and owner. In addition, the dog's help makes life a little easier for his owner and raises his stature as a valued companion to his family. It helps give the dog a purpose; it helps to keep his mind occupied and provides an outlet for his energy.

Backpacking is an exciting and healthful activity that the dog can be taught without assistance from more than his owner. The exercise of walking and climbing is good for man and dog alike, and the bond that they develop together is priceless. The rule of thumb is not to let the dog carry more than one-sixth of his body weight.

If you are interested in participating in organized competition with your German Shepherd, there are other activities other than obedience in which you and your dog can become involved. Agility is a popular and fun sport where dogs run through an obstacle course that includes various jumps, tunnels and other exercises to test the dog's speed and coordination. The owners run through the course beside their dogs to give commands and to guide them through the course. Although competitive, the focus is on fun— it's fun to do and fun to watch, as well as great exercise.

As a German Shepherd owner, you have the opportunity to participate in Schutzhund training if you choose. Schutzhund originated as a test to determine the best quality German Shepherds to be used for breeding stock. It is now used as a way to evaluate working ability and temperament, and some German Shepherd owners choose to train and compete with their dogs in Schutzhund trials. There are three levels of Schutzhund, ScH. I, SchH. II and SchH. III, each level being progressively more difficult to complete. Each level consists of training, obedience and protection phases. Training for Schutzhund is intense and must be practiced consistently to keep the dog keen. The experience of Schutzhund training is very rewarding for dog and owner, and the German Shepherd's tractability is well suited for this type of training.

REAP THE REWARDS

If you start with a normal, healthy dog and give him time, patience and some carefully executed lessons, you will reap the rewards of that training for the life of the dog. And what a life it will be! The two of you will find immeasurable pleasure in the companionship you have built together with love, respect and understanding.

MEDICAL PROBLEMS MOST FREQUENTLY SEEN IN GERMAN SHEPHERDS

Condition	Age of Onset	Cause	Area Affected
Acral Lick Dermatitis	Any age	Unknown	Legs
Aortic Stenosis	Young pups	Congenital	Heart
Cataracts	Young to middle age	Congenital	Eye
Demodicosis	Less than 18 mos	Possibly congenital	Skin
Elbow Dysplasia	4 to 7 mos	Congenital	Elbow joint
Epilepsy	1 to 3 years	Congenital	Nervous system
Exocrine Pancreatic Insufficiency	Less than 2 years	Congenital	Pancreas
Gastric Dilatation (Bloat)	Any age	Swallowing air	Stomach
Hip Dysplasia	By 2 years	Congenital	Hip joint
Hypertrophic Osteodystrophy	3 to 4 mos	Organism or vitamin imbalance	Bones
Hypothyroidism	1 to 3 years	Lymphocytic thyroiditis	Endocrine system
Panosteitis	Usually less than 1 year	Unknown	Leg bones
Pannus	Any age	Possibly congenital	Cornea
Von Willebrand's Disease	Birth	Congenital	Blood

HEALTH CARE OF YOUR
GERMAN SHEPHERD DOG

Dogs, being mammals like human beings, suffer from many of the same physical illnesses as people. They might even share many of the psychological problems. Since people usually know more about human diseases than canine maladies, many of the terms used in this chapter will be the familiar terms, not necessarily those used by veterinarians. We'll still use the term *x-ray*, instead of the more acceptable term *radiograph*. We will also use the familiar term *symptoms* even though dogs don't have symptoms. Dogs have *clinical signs*, because *symptoms* are verbal descriptions of what the patient feels is wrong. Since dogs can't speak, we have to look for clinical signs...but we still use the term *symptoms* in this book.

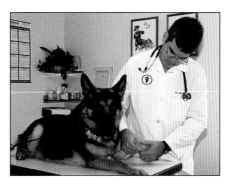

Your veterinarian will be your dog's friend throughout his life.

As a general rule, medicine is *practiced*. That term is not arbitrary. Medicine is an art. It is a constant changing art as we learn more and more about genetics, electronic aids (like CAT scans and MRIs). There are many dog maladies, like canine hip and elbow dysplasia, which are not universally treated. Some veterinarians opt for surgery more often than others.

SELECTING A QUALIFIED VETERINARIAN

Your selection of a veterinarian should be based not only upon his personality and skills with German Shepherds but also upon his convenience to your home. You want a vet who is close as you might have emergencies or need multiple visits for treatments. You

Your veterinarian's office should be a friendly, welcoming environment, staffed by caring professionals. Never compromise on your selection of a qualified vet.

want a vet who has services that you might require such as a boarding kennel, grooming facilities and tattooing, who makes sophisticated pet supplies available and who has a good reputation for ability and responsiveness. There is nothing more frustrating than having to wait a day or more to get a response from a veterinarian.

All veterinarians are licensed and their diplomas and/or certificates should be displayed in their waiting rooms. There are, however, many veterinary specialties that usually require further studies and internships. There are specialists in heart problems (veterinary cardiologists), skin problems (veterinary dermatologists), teeth and gum problems (veterinary dentists), eye problems (veterinary ophthalmologists) and x-rays (veterinary radiologists), and vets who have specialties in bones, muscles or certain organs. Most veterinarians do routine surgery such as neutering, stitching up wounds and docking tails for those breeds in which such is required.

When the problem affecting your dog is serious, it is not unusual or impudent to get another medical opinion. You might also want to compare costs between several veterinarians. Sophisticated health care and veterinary services can be very costly. Don't be bashful to discuss these costs. It is not infrequent that important decisions about the course of treatment to take are based upon financial considerations.

All veterinarians are licensed and all have been taught to read x-rays, but there are specialists called veterinary radiologists who are consulted for the fine details of x-ray interpretation.

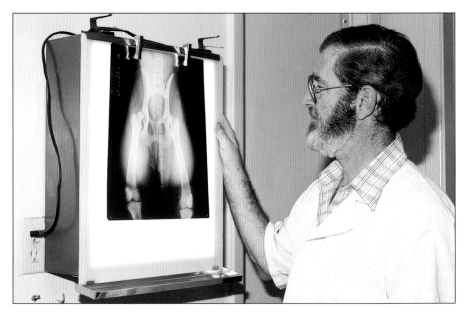

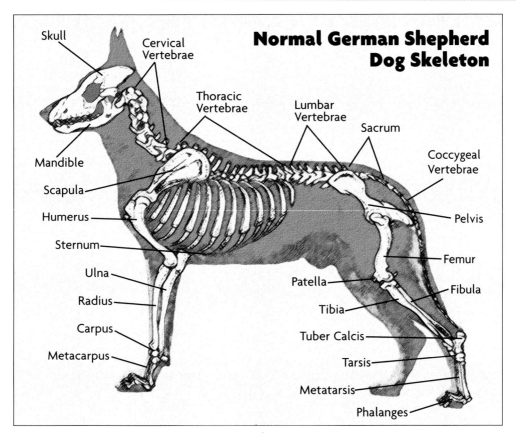

Normal German Shepherd Dog Skeleton

Skull · Cervical Vertebrae · Thoracic Vertebrae · Lumbar Vertebrae · Sacrum · Coccygeal Vertebrae · Mandible · Scapula · Humerus · Sternum · Ulna · Radius · Carpus · Metacarpus · Pelvis · Femur · Patella · Fibula · Tibia · Tuber Calcis · Tarsis · Metatarsis · Phalanges

PREVENTATIVE MEDICINE

It is much easier, less costly and more effective to practice preventative medicine than to fight bouts of illness and disease.

Properly bred puppies come from parents that were selected based upon their genetic-disease profiles. Their dam should have been vaccinated, free of all internal and external parasites and properly nourished. For these reasons, a visit to the veterinarian who cared for the dam is recommended. The dam can pass on disease resistance to her puppies. This resistance can last for eight to ten weeks. She can also pass on parasites and many infections, so it's worthwhile to learn as much about the dam's health as possible.

AFTER WEANING TO FIVE MONTHS OLD

Puppies should be weaned by the time they are about two months old. A puppy that remains for at least eight weeks with his mother and littermates usually adapts better to other dogs and people later in his life.

In every case, you should have your newly acquired puppy examined by a veterinarian immediately. Vaccination programs usually begin when the puppy is very young.

The puppy will have his teeth examined, have his skeletal conformation checked and have his general health checked prior to certification by the veterinarian. Many puppies have problems with their kneecaps, cataracts and other eye problems, heart murmurs and undescended testicles. They may also have personality problems and your veterinarian might have training in temperament evaluation. More dogs are abandoned because of behavioral problems than all other medical conditions combined.

Vaccination Scheduling

Most vaccinations are given by injection and should only be done by a veterinarian. Both he and you should keep a record of the date of the injection, the identification of the vaccine and the amount

DEWORMING

Ridding your puppy of worms is very important because they remove the nutrients that a growing puppy needs and certain worms that puppies carry, such as tapeworms and roundworms, can also infect humans.

Breeders initiate deworming programs at or about four weeks of age. The routine is repeated every two or three weeks until the puppy is three months old. The breeder from whom you obtained your puppy should provide you with the complete details of the deworming program.

Your veterinarian can prescribe and monitor the rest of the deworming program for you. The usual program is treating the puppy every 15–20 days until the puppy is positively worm-free. It is advised that you only treat your puppy with drugs that are recommended professionally.

given. Some vets give a first vaccination at eight weeks, but most breeders prefer not to commence until about ten weeks because of the risk of negating any antibodies passed on by the dam. The vaccination schedule is usually based on a 15-day cycle. Take your vet's advice as to when to vaccinate.

Most vaccinations immunize your puppy against viruses. The usual vaccines contain immunizing doses of several different viruses such as distemper,

Vaccinations are extremely important, as infectious diseases can easily be passed from dog to dog.

HEALTH AND VACCINATION SCHEDULE

AGE IN WEEKS:	3RD	6TH	8TH	10TH	12TH	14TH	16TH	20-24TH
Worm Control	✔	✔	✔	✔	✔	✔	✔	✔
Neutering								✔
Heartworm		✔						✔
Parvovirus		✔		✔		✔		✔
Distemper			✔		✔		✔	
Hepatitis			✔		✔		✔	
Leptospirosis		✔		✔		✔		
Parainfluenza		✔		✔		✔		
Dental Examination			✔					✔
Complete Physical			✔					✔
Temperament Testing			✔					
Coronavirus					✔			
Canine Cough		✔						
Hip Dysplasia							✔	
Rabies								✔

Vaccinations are not instantly effective. It takes about two weeks for the dog's immune system to develop antibodies. Most vaccinations require annual booster shots. Your veterinarian should guide you in this regard.

parvovirus, parainfluenza and hepatitis. There are other vaccines available when the puppy is at risk. You should rely upon professional advice. This is especially true for the booster-shot program. Most vaccination programs require a booster when the puppy is a year old, and once a year thereafter. In some cases, circumstances may require more or less frequent immunizations.

Canine cough (or kennel cough), more formally known as tracheobronchitis, is treated with a vaccine which is sprayed into the dog's nostrils. The effectiveness of a parvovirus vaccination program can be tested to be certain that the vaccinations are protective. Your veterinarian will explain and manage these and all of the other details of vaccinations.

FIVE MONTHS TO ONE YEAR OF AGE
By the time your puppy is five months old, he should have completed his vaccination program. During his physical examination, he should be evaluated for hip and elbow dysplasia plus other diseases of the joints. There are tests to assist in the prediction of these problems. As previously mentioned, other tests can also be

Most German Shepherds are fairly adaptable to a variety of climates, though they do not relish the humid weather. Heat-stroke is a serious problem for all working dogs and precautions to keep your dog cool will be appreciated.

run, such as the parvovirus antibody titer, which can assess the effectiveness of the vaccination program.

Unless you intend to breed or show your dog, neutering the puppy around six months of age is recommended. Discuss this with your veterinarian. Most professionals advise neutering puppies that will be solely companion animals. Responsible breeders will sell pet-quality puppies on the condition that they are neutered (males) or spayed (females). This clause will be a part of the breeder's sales agreement.

Neutering and spaying have proven to be extremely beneficial to both male and female dogs. Besides the obvious impossibility of pregnancy in females, it inhibits (but does not prevent) breast cancer in bitches and

prevents prostate cancer in male dogs.

Blood tests are performed for heartworm infestation and it is possible that your puppy will be placed on a preventative therapy that will prevent heartworm infection as well as control other internal parasites.

OLDER THAN ONE YEAR

Continue to visit the veterinarian at least once a year. There is no such disease as *old age*, but bodily functions do change with age, and the eyes and ears are no longer as efficient. Neither are the internal workings of the liver, kidneys and intestines. Proper dietary changes, recommended by your veterinarian, can make life more pleasant for the aging German Shepherd Dog and you.

SKIN PROBLEMS IN GERMAN SHEPHERD DOGS

Veterinarians are consulted by dog owners for skin problems more than for any other group of diseases or maladies. Dogs' skin is almost as sensitive as human skin and both suffer almost the same maladies, though the occurrence of acne in most breeds is rare! For this reason, veterinary dermatology has developed into a specialty practiced by many veterinarians.

Since many skin problems have visual symptoms that are almost identical, it requires the skill of an

DENTAL HEALTH

A dental examination is in order when the dog is between six months and one year of age so that any permanent teeth that have erupted incorrectly can be corrected. Durable nylon and safe edible chews should be a part of your puppy's arsenal for good health, good teeth and pleasant breath. The vast majority of dogs three to four years old and older has diseases of the gums from lack of dental attention. Using the various types of dental chews can be very effective in controlling dental plaque.

experienced veterinary dermatologist to identify and cure many of the more severe skin disorders. Pet shops sell many treatments for skin problems, but most of the treatments are simply directed at symptoms and not the underlying problem(s). Simply put, if your dog is suffering from a skin disorder, seek professional assistance as quickly as possible. As with all diseases, the earlier a problem is identified and treated, the more likely that the cure will be successful.

HEREDITARY SKIN DISORDERS

Veterinary dermatologists are currently researching a number of skin disorders that are believed to have a hereditary basis. These inherited diseases are transmitted by both parents, who appear (phenotypically) normal but have a recessive gene for the disease, meaning that they carry, but are not affected by, the disease. These diseases pose serious problems to breeders because in some instances there are no methods of identifying carriers. Often the secondary diseases associated with these skin conditions are even more debilitating than the skin disorders themselves, including cancers and respiratory problems.

Among the hereditary skin disorders, for which the mode of inheritance is known, are cutaneous asthenia (Ehlers-Danlos syndrome), which has been cited in the German Shepherd; sebaceous adenitis, which is most commonly seen in Standard Poodles, though has been cited in the breed; cyclic hematopoiesis; dermatomyositis; IgA deficiency, also cited in the breed and is marked by recurrent infections in the urinary tract, respiratory tract and skin; acrodermatitis; color dilution alopecia and nodular dermatofibrosis, which is most

Dogs who spend times in woodsy areas are prone to parasites and other possible skin problems.

commonly seen in this breed and has been cited since the late 1960s. All inherited diseases must be diagnosed and treated by a veterinary specialist. Of all these diseases, nodular dermatofibrosis is the one about which Shepherd folk are most concerned, and any dog with lumps on his legs should be examined by a vet. Affected dogs develop tumors in the kidneys and/or uterus, which can be removed before the cancer spreads. It should be noted that since German Shepherds are so populous around the world, more veterinary data exists on the breed than on most other breeds. A high incidence of certain hereditary diseases therefore must be viewed in perspective, though the seriousness of these life-threatening hereditary diseases should not be dismissed.

PARASITE BITES

Many of us are allergic to mosquito bites. The bites itch, erupt and may even become infected. Dogs have the same reaction to fleas, ticks and/or mites. When you feel the prick of the mosquito when it bites you, you have a chance to kill it with your hand. Unfortunately, when your dog is bitten by a flea, tick or mite, it can only scratch it away or bite it. By the time the dog has been bitten, the parasite has done some of its damage. It may also have laid eggs to cause further

DO YOU KNOW ABOUT HIP DYSPLASIA?

Hip dysplasia is a fairly common condition found in German Shepherd Dogs, as well as other large breeds. When a dog has hip dysplasia, his hind leg has an incorrectly formed hip joint. By constant use of the hip joint, it becomes more and more loose, wears abnormally and may become arthritic.

Hip dysplasia can only be confirmed with an x-ray, but certain symptoms may indicate a problem. Your German Shepherd Dog may have a hip dysplasia problem if he walks in a peculiar manner, hops instead of smoothly running, uses his hinds legs in unison (to keep the pressure off the weak joint), has trouble getting up from a prone position and always sits with both legs together on one side of his body.

As the dog matures, he may adapt well to life with a bad hip, but in a few years the arthritis develops and many German Shepherd Dogs with hip dysplasia become cripples.

Hip dysplasia is considered an inherited disease and can usually be predicted when the dog is four to nine months old, and diagnosed definitely at two years old. Some experts claim that a special diet might help your puppy outgrow the bad hip, but the usual treatments are surgical. The removal of the pectineus muscle, the removal of the round part of the femur, reconstructing the pelvis and replacing the hip with an artificial one. All of these surgical interventions are expensive, but they are usually very successful. Follow the advice of your veterinarian.

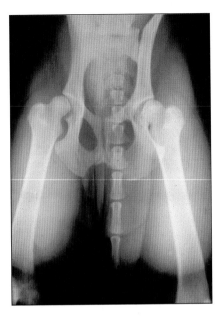

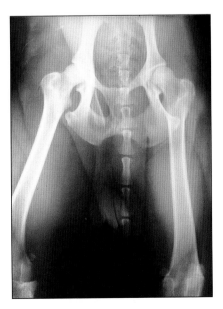

Compare the two hip joints and you'll understand dysplasia. Hip dysplasia is a badly worn hip joint caused by improper fit of the bone into the socket. It is the most common joint problem in German Shepherd Dogs.

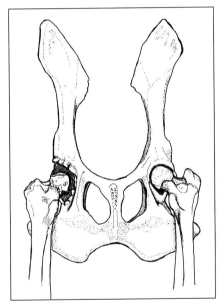

The healthy hip joint on the right and the unhealthy hip joint on the left.

Hip dysplasia can only be positively diagnosed by x-ray. German Shepherd Dogs manifest the problem when they are between four and nine months of age, the so-called fast-growth period. A diagnosis of dysplasia or a clearance for non-dysplastic hips can be issued at two years of age based on x-ray examinations.

problems in the near future. The itching from parasite bites is probably due to the saliva injected into the site when the parasite sucks the dog's blood.

AIRBORNE ALLERGIES

Just as humans have hay fever, rose fever and other fevers from which they suffer during the pollinating season, many dogs suffer from the same inhalent allergies. The German Shepherd exhibits a high incidence of atopy or hay fever. So when the pollen

count is high, your dog might suffer. However, don't expect him to sneeze and have a runny nose as a human would. Dogs react to pollen allergies the same way they react to fleas—they scratch and bite themselves. German Shepherd Dogs are very susceptible to airborne pollen allergies.

Dogs, like humans, can be tested for allergens. Discuss the testing with your veterinary dermatologist.

FOOD PROBLEMS

Dogs can be allergic to many foods that are best-sellers and highly recommended by breeders and veterinarians. Changing the brand of food that you buy may not eliminate the problem because the element of the food to which the dog is allergic may also be contained in the new brand.

Recognizing a food allergy is difficult. Humans vomit or have rashes when they eat a food to which they are allergic. Dogs neither vomit nor (usually) develop a rash. Instead they itch, scratch and bite, thus making the diagnosis extremely difficult. While pollen allergies and parasite bites are usually seasonal, food allergies are year-round problems.

TREATING FOOD PROBLEMS

Handling food allergies and food intolerance yourself is possible. Put your dog on a diet that he has never had. Obviously, if he has never eaten this new food,

THE SAME ALLERGIES

Chances are that you and your dog will have the same allergies. Your allergies are readily recognizable and usually easily treated. Your dog's allergies may be masked.

he can't have been allergic or intolerant of it. Start with a single ingredient that is *not* in the dog's diet at the present time. Ingredients like beef or chicken are common in dog's diets, so try something more exotic like fish, rabbit, pheasant or some other quality source of protein. Keep the dog on this diet (with no additives) for a month. If the symptoms of food allergy or intolerance disappear, chances are that you have defined the cause.

Don't think that the single ingredient cured the problem. You still must find a suitable diet and ascertain which ingredient in the old diet was objectionable. This is most easily done by adding ingredients to the new diet one at a time until the problem is solved. Let the dog stay on the modified diet for a month before you add another ingredient.

An alternative method is to identify the main ingredient in the dog's original diet and eliminate the main ingredient by buying a different food that does not have that ingredient. Keep experimenting until the symptoms disappear after one month on the new diet.

DETECTING BLOAT

As important as it is to take precautions against bloat/gastric torsion, it is of equal importance to recognize the symptoms. It is necessary for your German Shepherd to get immediate veterinary attention if you notice any of the following signs:

- Your dog's stomach starts to distend, ending up large and as tight as a football;
- Your dog is dribbling, as no saliva can be swallowed;
- Your dog makes frequent attempts to vomit but cannot bring anything up due to the stomach's being closed off;
- Your dog is distressed from pain;
- Your dog starts to suffer from clinical shock, meaning that there is not enough blood in the dog's circulation as the hard, dilated stomach stops the blood from returning to the heart to be pumped around the body. Clinical shock is indicated by pale gums and tongue, as they have been starved of blood. The shocked dog also has glazed, staring eyes.

You have minutes, yes *minutes,* to get your dog into surgery. If you see any of these symptoms at any time of the day or night, get to the vet immediately. Someone will have to phone and warn that you are on your way (which is a justification for the invention of the cellular phone!), so that they can be prepared to get your pet on the operating table.

A male dog flea, *Ctenocephalides canis.*

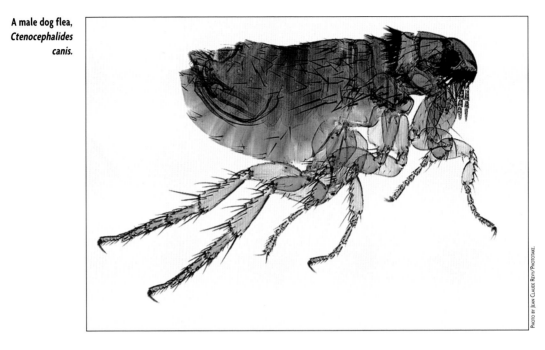

PHOTO BY JEAN CLAUDE REVY/PHOTOTAKE.

EXTERNAL PARASITES

FLEAS

Of all the problems to which dogs are prone, none is more well known and frustrating than fleas. Flea infestation is relatively simple to cure but difficult to prevent. Parasites that are harbored inside the body are a bit more difficult to eradicate but they are easier to control.

To control flea infestation, you have to understand the flea's life cycle. Fleas are often thought of as a summertime problem, but centrally heated homes have changed the patterns and fleas can be found at any time of the year. The most effective method of flea control is a two-stage approach: one stage to kill the adult fleas, and the other to control the development of pre-adult fleas. Unfortunately, no single active ingredient is effective against all stages of the life cycle.

FLEA KILLER CAUTION— "POISON"

Flea-killers are poisonous. You should not spray these toxic chemicals on areas of a dog's body that he licks, including his genitals and his face. Flea killers taken internally are a better answer, but check with your vet in case internal therapy is not advised for your dog.

LIFE CYCLE STAGES

During its life, a flea will pass through four life stages: egg, larva, pupa or nymph and adult. The adult stage is the most visible and irritating stage of the flea life cycle, and this is why the majority of flea-control products concentrate on this stage. The fact is that adult fleas account for only 1% of the total flea population, and the other 99% exist in pre-adult stages, i.e., eggs, larvae and nymphs. The pre-adult stages are barely visible to the naked eye.

THE LIFE CYCLE OF THE FLEA

Eggs are laid on the dog, usually in quantities of about 20 or 30, several times a day. The adult female flea must have a blood meal before each egg-laying session. When first laid, the eggs will cling to the dog's hair, as the eggs are still moist. However, they will quickly dry out and fall from the dog, especially if the dog moves around or scratches. Many eggs will fall off in the dog's favorite area or an area in which he spends a lot of time, such as his bed.

Once the eggs fall from the dog onto the carpet or furniture, they will hatch into larvae. This takes from one to ten days. Larvae are not particularly mobile and will usually travel only a few inches from where they hatch. However, they do have a tendency to move away from bright light and heavy

> ***EN GARDE:***
> **CATCHING FLEAS OFF GUARD!**
> Consider the following ways to arm yourself against fleas:
> - Add a small amount of pennyroyal or eucalyptus oil to your dog's bath. These natural remedies repel fleas.
> - Supplement your dog's food with fresh garlic (minced or grated) and a hearty amount of brewer's yeast, both of which ward off fleas.
> - Use a flea comb on your dog daily. Submerge fleas in a cup of bleach to kill them quickly.
> - Confine the dog to only a few rooms to limit the spread of fleas in the home.
> - Vacuum daily...and get all of the crevices! Dispose of the bag every few days until the problem is under control.
> - Wash your dog's bedding daily. Cover cushions where your dog sleeps with towels, and wash the towels often.

traffic—under furniture and behind doors are common places to find high quantities of flea larvae.

The flea larvae feed on dead organic matter, including adult flea feces, until they are ready to change into adult fleas. Fleas will usually remain as larvae for around seven days. After this period, the larvae will pupate into protective pupae. While inside the pupae, the larvae will undergo metamorphosis and change into adult fleas. This can take as little time as a few days, but the adult fleas can remain inside the pupae waiting to hatch for up to two years. The pupae are signaled to hatch by certain stimuli, such as physical pressure—the pupae's being stepped on, heat from an animal's lying on the pupae or increased carbon-dioxide levels and vibrations—indicating that a suitable host is available.

Once hatched, the adult flea must feed within a few days. Once the adult flea finds a host, it will not leave voluntarily. It only becomes dislodged by grooming or the host animal's scratching.

The adult flea will remain on the host for the duration of its life unless forcibly removed.

TREATING THE ENVIRONMENT AND THE DOG

Treating fleas should be a two-pronged attack. First, the environment needs to be treated; this includes carpets and furniture, especially the dog's bedding and areas underneath furniture. The environment should be treated with a household spray containing an Insect Growth Regulator (IGR) and an insecticide to kill the adult fleas. Most IGRs are effective against eggs and larvae; they actually mimic the fleas' own hormones and stop the eggs and larvae from developing into adult fleas. There are currently no treatments available to attack the pupa stage of the life cycle, so the adult insecticide is used to kill the newly hatched adult fleas before they find a host. Most IGRs are active for many months, while

A scanning electron micrograph of a dog or cat flea, *Ctenocephalides*, magnified more than 100x. This image has been colorized for effect.

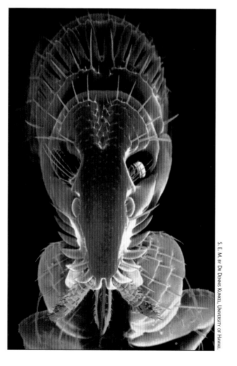

THE LIFE CYCLE OF THE FLEA

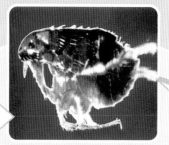

Adult

Egg

**Pupa
or
Nymph**

Larva

PHOTOS COURTESY OF FLEABUSTERS® RX FOR FLEAS.

A LOOK AT FLEAS
Fleas have been around for millions of years and have adapted to
changing host animals. They are able to go through a complete life cycle
in less than one month or they can extend their lives to almost two years
by remaining as pupae or cocoons. They do not need blood or any other
food for up to 20 months.

INSECT GROWTH REGULATOR (IGR)

Two types of products should be used when treating fleas—a product to treat the pet and a product to treat the home. Adult fleas represent less than 1% of the flea population. The pre-adult fleas (eggs, larvae and pupae) represent more than 99% of the flea population and are found in the environment; it is in the case of pre-adult fleas that products containing an Insect Growth Regulator (IGR) should be used in the home.

IGRs are a new class of compounds used to prevent the development of insects. They do not kill the insect outright, but instead use the insect's biology against it to stop it from completing its growth. Products that contain methoprene are the world's first and leading IGRs. Used to control fleas and other insects, this type of IGR will stop flea larvae from developing and protect the house for up to seven months.

The American dog tick, Dermacentor variabilis, is probably the most common tick found on dogs. Look at the strength in its eight legs! No wonder it's hard to detach them.

The second stage of treatment is to apply an adult insecticide to the dog. Traditionally, this would be in the form of a collar or a spray, but more recent innovations include digestible insecticides that poison the fleas when they ingest the dog's blood. Alternatively, there are drops that, when placed on the back of the dog's neck, spread throughout the hair and skin to kill adult fleas.

TICKS

Though not as common as fleas, ticks are found all over the tropical and temperate world. They don't bite, like fleas; they harpoon. They dig their sharp proboscis (nose) into the dog's skin and drink the blood. Their

adult insecticides are only active for a few days.

When treating with a household spray, it is a good idea to vacuum before applying the product. This stimulates as many pupae as possible to hatch into adult fleas. The vacuum cleaner should also be treated with an insecticide to prevent the eggs and larvae that have been collected in the vacuum bag from hatching.

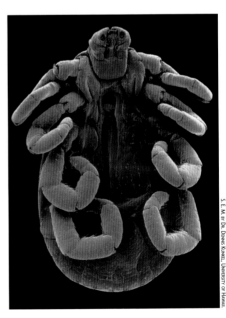

only food and drink is dog's blood. Dogs can get Lyme disease, Rocky Mountain spotted fever, tick bite paralysis and many other diseases from ticks. They may live where fleas are found and they like to hide in cracks or seams in walls. They are controlled the same way fleas are controlled.

The American dog tick, *Dermacentor variabilis*, may well be the most common dog tick in many geographical areas, especially those areas where the climate is hot and humid. Most dog ticks have life expectancies of a week to six months, depending upon climatic conditions. They can neither jump nor fly, but they can crawl slowly and can range up to 16 feet to reach a sleeping or unsuspecting dog.

MITES

Just as fleas and ticks can be problematic for your dog, mites can also lead to an itchy nuisance. Microscopic in size, mites are related to ticks and generally take up permanent residence on their host animal—in this case, your dog! The term *mange* refers to any infestation caused by one of the mighty mites, of which there are six varieties that concern dog owners.

Demodex mites cause a condition known as demodicosis

DEER-TICK CROSSING

The great outdoors may be fun for your dog, but it also is a home to dangerous ticks. Deer ticks carry a bacterium known as *Borrelia burgdorferi* and are most active in the autumn and spring. When infections are caught early, penicillin and tetracycline are effective antibiotics, but if left untreated the bacteria may cause neurological, kidney and cardiac problems as well as long-term trouble with walking and painful joints.

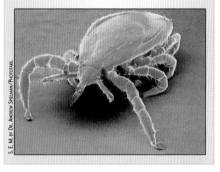

S. E. M. BY DR. ANDREW SPIELMAN/PHOTOTAKE.

PHOTO BY DR. DENNIS KUNKEL, UNIVERSITY OF HAWAII.

The head of an American dog tick, *Dermacentor variabilis*, enlarged and colorized for effect.

The mange mite, *Psoroptes bovis*, can infest cattle and other domestic animals.

Photo by James Hayden/Yoav/Phototake.

(sometimes called red mange or follicular mange), in which the mites live in the dog's hair follicles and sebaceous glands. This type of mange is commonly passed from the dam to her puppies and usually shows up on the puppies' muzzles, though demodicosis is not transferable from one normal dog to another. Most dogs recover from this type of mange without any treatment, though topical therapies are commonly prescribed by the vet.

The *Cheyletiellosis* mite is the

Human lice look like dog lice; the two are closely related.

Photo by Dwight R. Kuhn.

hook-mouthed culprit associated with "walking dandruff," a condition that affects dogs as well as cats and rabbits. This mite lives on the surface of the animal's skin and is readily transferable through direct or indirect contact with an affected animal. The dandruff is present in the form of scaly skin, which may or may not be itchy. If not treated, this mange can affect a whole kennel of dogs and can be spread to humans as well.

The *Sarcoptes* mite causes intense itching on the dog in the form of a condition known as scabies or sarcoptic mange. The cycle of the *Sarcoptes* mite lasts about three weeks, and the mites live in the top layer of the dog's skin (epidermis), preferably in areas with little hair. Scabies is highly contagious and can be passed to humans. Sometimes an allergic reaction to the mite worsens the severe itching associated with sarcoptic mange.

Ear mites, *Otodectes cynotis,* lead to otodectic mange, which most commonly affects the outer ear canal of the dog, though other areas can be affected as well. Dogs with ear-mite infestation commonly scratch at their ears, causing further irritation, and shake their heads. Dark brown droppings in the outer ear confirm the diagnosis. Your vet can prescribe a treatment to flush out the ears and kill any eggs in the ears. A complete month of treatment is necessary to cure the mange.

Two other mites, less common in dogs, include *Dermanyssus gallinae* (the poultry or red mite) and *Eutrombicula alfreddugesi* (the North American mite associated with trombiculidiasis or chigger infestation). The poultry mite frequently lives on chickens, but can transfer to dogs who spend time near farm animals. Chigger

DO NOT MIX

Never mix pest control products without first consulting your vet. Some products can become toxic when combined with others and can cause fatal consequences.

NOT A DROP TO DRINK

Never allow your dog to swim in polluted water or public areas where water quality can be suspect. Even perfectly clear water can harbour parasites, many of which can cause serious to fatal illnesses in canines. Areas inhabited by waterfowl and other wildlife are especially dangerous.

infestation affects dogs in the Central US who have exposure to woodlands. The types of mange caused by both of these mites are treatable by veterinarians.

INTERNAL PARASITES

Most animals—fishes, birds and mammals, including dogs and humans—have worms and other parasites that live inside their bodies. According to Dr. Herbert R. Axelrod, the fish pathologist, there are two kinds of parasites: dumb and smart. The smart parasites live in peaceful cooperation with their hosts (symbiosis), while the dumb parasites kill their hosts. Most worm infections are relatively easy to control. If they are not controlled, they weaken the host dog to the point that other medical problems occur, but they do not kill the host as dumb parasites would.

A brown dog tick, *Rhipicephalus sanguineus*, is an uncommon but annoying tick found on dogs.

PHOTO BY CAROLINA BIOLOGICAL SUPPLY/PHOTOTAKE.

The roundworm *Rhabditis* can infect both dogs and humans.

The roundworm, *Ascaris lumbricoides.*

ROUNDWORMS

Average-size dogs can pass 1,360,000 roundworm eggs every day. For example, if there were only 1 million dogs in the world, the world would be saturated with thousands of tons of dog feces. These feces would contain around 15,000,000,000 roundworm eggs.

Up to 31% of home yards and children's sand boxes in the US contain roundworm eggs.

Flushing dog's feces down the toilet is not a safe practice because the usual sewage treatments do not destroy roundworm eggs.

Infected puppies start shedding roundworm eggs at three weeks of age. They can be infected by their mother's milk.

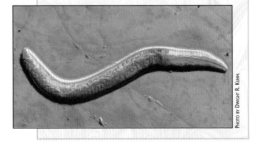

PHOTO BY DWIGHT R. KUHN.

ROUNDWORMS

The roundworms that infect dogs are known scientifically as *Toxocara canis.* They live in the dog's intestines and shed eggs continually. It has been estimated that a dog produces about 6 or more ounces of feces every day. Each ounce of feces averages hundreds of thousands of roundworm eggs. There are no known areas in which dogs roam that do not contain roundworm eggs. The greatest danger of roundworms is that they infect people, too! It is wise to have your dog tested regularly for round-worms.

In young puppies, roundworms cause bloated bellies, diarrhea, coughing and vomiting, and are transmitted from the dam (through blood or milk). Affected puppies will not appear as animated as normal puppies. The worms appear spaghetti-like, measuring as long as 6 inches. Adult dogs can acquire roundworms through coprophagia (eating contaminated feces) or by killing rodents that carry roundworms.

Roundworm infection can kill puppies and cause severe problems in adults, as the hatched larvae travel to the lungs and trachea through the bloodstream. Cleanliness is the best preventative for roundworms. Always pick up after your dog and dispose of feces in appropriate receptacles.

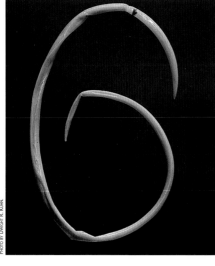

PHOTO BY DWIGHT R. KUHN

HOOKWORMS

In the United States, dog owners have to be concerned about four different species of hookworm, the most common and most serious of which is *Ancylostoma caninum,* which prefers warm climates. The others are *Ancylostoma braziliense, Ancylostoma tubaeforme* and *Uncinaria stenocephala,* the latter of which is a concern to dogs living in the Northern US and Canada, as this species prefers cold climates. Hookworms are dangerous to humans as well as to dogs and cats, and can be the cause of severe anemia due to iron deficiency. The worm uses its teeth to attach itself to the dog's intestines and changes the site of its attachment about six times per day. Each time the worm repositions itself, the dog loses

blood and can become anemic. *Ancylostoma caninum* is the most likely of the four species to cause anemia in the dog.

Symptoms of hookworm infection include dark stools, weight loss, general weakness, pale coloration and anemia, as well as possible skin problems. Fortunately, hookworms are easily purged from the affected dog with a number of medications that have proven effective. Discuss these with your veterinarian. Most heartworm preventatives include a hookworm insecticide as well.

Owners also must be aware that hookworms can infect humans, who can acquire the larvae through exposure to contaminated feces. Since the worms cannot complete their life cycle on a human, the worms simply infest the skin and cause irritation. This condition is known as cutaneous larva migrans syndrome. As a preventative, use disposable gloves or a "poop-scoop" to pick up your dog's droppings and prevent your dog (or neighborhood cats) from defecating in children's play areas.

The hookworm *Ancylostoma caninum.*

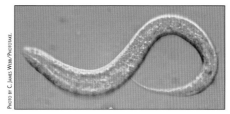

PHOTO BY C. JAMES WEBB/PHOTOTAKE

The infective stage of the hookworm larva.

TAPEWORMS

Humans, rats, squirrels, foxes, coyotes, wolves and domestic dogs are all susceptible to tapeworm infection. Except in humans, tapeworms are usually not a fatal infection. Infected individuals can harbor 1000 parasitic worms.

Tapeworms, like some other types of worm, are hermaphroditic, meaning male and female in the same worm.

If dogs eat infected rats or mice, or anything else injected with tapeworm, they get the tapeworm disease. One month after attaching to a dog's intestine, the worm starts shedding eggs. These eggs are infective immediately. Infective eggs can live for a few months without a host animal.

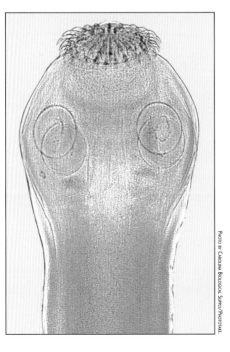

The head and rostellum (the round prominence on the scolex) of a tapeworm, which infects dogs and humans.

PHOTO BY CAROLINA BIOLOGICAL SUPPLY/PHOTOTAKE.

TAPEWORMS

There are many species of tapeworm, all of which are carried by fleas! The most common tapeworm affecting dogs is known as *Dipylidium caninum*. The dog eats the flea and starts the tapeworm cycle. Humans can also be infected with tapeworms—so don't eat fleas! Fleas are so small that your dog could pass them onto your hands, your plate or your food and thus make it possible for you to ingest a flea that is carrying tapeworm eggs.

While tapeworm infection is not life-threatening in dogs (smart parasite!), it can be the cause of a very serious liver disease for humans. About 50% of the humans infected with *Echinococcus multilocularis*, a type of tapeworm that causes alveolar hydatid, perish.

WHIPWORMS

In North America, whipworms are counted among the most common parasitic worms in dogs. The whipworm's scientific name is *Trichuris vulpis*. These worms attach themselves in the lower parts of the intestine, where they feed. Affected dogs may only experience upset tummies, colic and diarrhea. These worms, however, can live for months or years in the dog, beginning their larval stage in the small intestine, spending their adult stage in the large intestine and finally passing infective eggs through the dog's feces. The only way to detect whipworms is through a fecal examination, though this is not always foolproof. Treatment for whipworms is tricky, due to the worms' unusual life-cycle pattern, and very often dogs are reinfected due to exposure to infective eggs on the ground. The whipworm eggs can survive in the environment for as long as five years, thus cleaning up droppings in your own backyard as well as in public places is absolutely essential for sanitation purposes and the health of your dog.

THREADWORMS
Though less common than roundworms, hookworms and those listed above, threadworms concern dog owners in the Southwestern US and Gulf Coast area where the climate is hot and humid. Living in the small intestine of the dog, this worm measures a mere 2 millimeters and is round in shape. Like that of the whipworm, the threadworm's life cycle is very complex and the eggs and larvae are passed through the feces. A deadly disease in humans, *Strongyloides* readily infects people, and the handling of feces is the most common means of transmission. Threadworms are most often seen in young puppies; bloody diarrhea and pneumonia are symptoms. Sick puppies must be isolated and treated immediately; vets recommend a follow-up treatment one month later.

HEARTWORM PREVENTATIVES

There are many heartworm preventatives on the market, many of which are sold at your veterinarian's office. These products can be given daily or monthly, depending on the manufacturer's instructions. All of these preventatives contain chemical insecticides directed at killing heartworms, which leads to some controversy among dog owners. In effect, heartworm preventatives are necessary evils, though you should determine how necessary based on your pet's lifestyle. There is no doubt that heartworm is a dreadful disease that threatens the life of dogs. However, the likelihood of your dog's being bitten by an infected mosquito is slim in most places, and a mosquito-repellent (or an herbal remedy such as Wormwood or Black Walnut) is much safer for your dog and will not compromise his immune system (the way heartworm preventatives will). Should you decide to use the traditional preventative "medications," you can consider giving the pill every other or third month. Since the toxins in the pill will kill the heartworms at all stages of development, the pill would be effective in killing larvae, nymphs or adults and it takes four months for the larvae to reach the adult stage. Thus, there is no rationale to poisoning the dog's system on a monthly basis. Lastly, do not give the pill during the winter months since there are no mosquitoes around to pass on their infection, unless you live in a tropical environment.

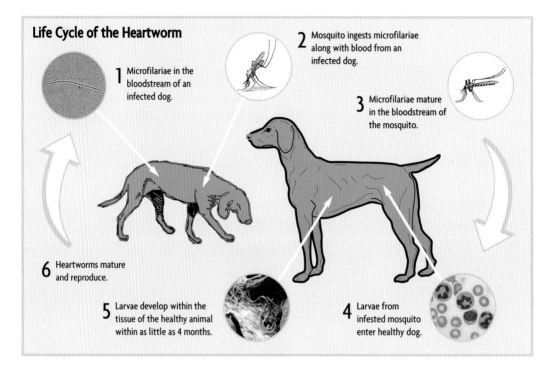

Life Cycle of the Heartworm

1 Microfilariae in the bloodstream of an infected dog.

2 Mosquito ingests microfilariae along with blood from an infected dog.

3 Microfilariae mature in the bloodstream of the mosquito.

4 Larvae from infested mosquito enter healthy dog.

5 Larvae develop within the tissue of the healthy animal within as little as 4 months.

6 Heartworms mature and reproduce.

HEARTWORMS

Heartworms are thin, extended worms up to 12 inches long, which live in a dog's heart and the major blood vessels surrounding it. Dogs may have up to 200 worms. Symptoms may be loss of energy, loss of appetite, coughing, the development of a pot belly and anemia.

Heartworms are transmitted by mosquitoes. The mosquito drinks the blood of an infected dog and takes in larvae with the blood. The larvae, called microfilariae, develop within the body of the mosquito and are passed on to the next dog bitten after the larvae mature. It takes two to three weeks for the larvae to develop to the infective stage within the body of the mosquito. Dogs are usually treated at about six weeks of age and maintained on a prophylactic dose given monthly.

Blood testing for heartworms is not necessarily indicative of how seriously your dog is infected. Although this is a dangerous disease, it is not easy for a dog to be infected. Discuss the various preventatives with your vet, as there are many different types now available. Together you can decide on a safe course of prevention for your dog.

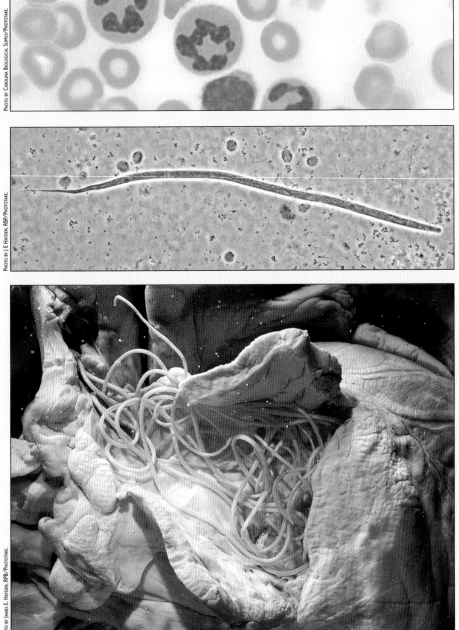

Magnified heartworm larvae, *Dirofilaria immitis.*

Heartworm, *Dirofilaria immitis.*

The heart of a dog infected with canine heartworm, *Dirofilaria immitis.*

HOMEOPATHY:
an alternative
to conventional
medicine

"Less is Most"

Using this principle, the strength of a homeopathic remedy is measured by the number of serial dilutions that were undertaken to create it. The greater the number of serial dilutions, the greater the strength of the homeopathic remedy. The potency of a remedy that has been made by making a dilution of 1 part in 100 parts (or 1/100) is 1c or 1cH. If this remedy is subjected to a series of further dilutions, each one being 1/100, a more dilute and stronger remedy is produced. If the remedy is diluted in this way six times, it is called 6c or 6cH. A dilution of 6c is 1 part in 1000,000,000,000. In general, higher potencies in more frequent doses are better for acute symptoms and lower potencies in more infrequent doses are more useful for chronic, long-standing problems.

CURING OUR DOGS NATURALLY

Holistic medicine means treating the whole animal as a unique, perfect living being. Generally, holistic treatments do not suppress the symptoms that the body naturally produces, as do most medications prescribed by conventional doctors and vets. Holistic methods seek to cure disease by regaining balance and harmony in the patient's environment. Some of these methods include use of nutritional therapy, herbs, flower essences, aromatherapy, acupuncture, massage, chiropractic and, of course the most popular holistic approach, homeopathy.

Homeopathy is a theory or system of treating illness with small doses of substances which, if administered in larger quantities, would produce the symptoms that the patient already has. This approach is often described as "like cures like." Although modern veterinary medicine is geared toward the "quick fix," homeopathy relies on the belief that, given the time, the body is able to heal itself and return to its natural, healthy state.

Choosing a remedy to cure a problem in our dogs is the difficult part of homeopathy. Consult with your veterinarian for a professional diagnosis of your dog's symptoms.

Often these symptoms require immediate conventional care. If your vet is willing and knowledgeable, you may attempt a homeopathic remedy. Be aware that cortisone prevents homeopathic remedies from working. There are hundreds of possibilities and combinations to cure many problems in dogs, from basic physical problems such as excessive shedding, fleas or other parasites, unattractive doggy odor, bad breath, obesity, upset tummy, dry, oily or dull coat, diarrhea, ear problems or eye discharge (including tears and dry or mucousy matter), to behavioral abnormalities such as fear of loud noises, habitual licking, poor appetite, excessive barking and various phobias. From alumina to zincum metallicum, the remedies span the planet and the imagination...from flowers and weeds to chemicals, insect droppings, diesel smoke and volcanic ash.

Using "Like to Treat Like"

Unlike conventional medicines that suppress symptoms, homeopathic remedies treat illnesses with small doses of substances that, if administered in larger quantities, would produce the symptoms that the patient already has. While the same homeopathic remedy can be used to treat different symptoms in different dogs, here are some interesting remedies and their uses.

Apis Mellifica
(made from honey bee venom) can be used for allergies or to reduce swelling that occurs in acutely infected kidneys.

Diesel Smoke
can be used to help control travel sickness.

Calcarea Fluorica
(made from calcium fluoride, which helps harden bone structure) can be useful in treating hard lumps in tissues.

Natrum Muriaticum
(made from common salt, sodium chloride) is useful in treating thin, thirsty dogs.

Nitricum Acidum
(made from nitric acid) is used for symptoms you would expect to see from contact with acids such as lesions, especially where the skin joins the linings of body orifices or openings such as the lips and nostrils.

Symphytum
(made from the herb Knitbone, *Symphytum officianale)* is used to encourage bones to heal.

Urtica Urens
(made from the common stinging nettle) is used in treating painful, irritating rashes.

A little gray around the muzzle doesn't keep the senior German Shepherd from being a loyal and loving pet.

YOUR SENIOR
GERMAN SHEPHERD DOG

The term *old* is a qualitative term. For dogs, as well as for their masters, old is relative. Certainly we can all distinguish between a puppy German Shepherd and an adult German Shepherd—there are the obvious physical traits, such as size, appearance and facial expressions, and personality traits. Puppies and young dogs like to play with children. Children's natural exuberance is a good match for the seemingly endless energy of young dogs. They like to run, jump, chase and retrieve. When dogs grow older and cease their interaction with children, they are often thought of as being too old to keep pace with the kids. On the other hand, if an German Shepherd is only exposed to people with quieter lifestyles, his life will normally be less active and the decrease in his activity level as he ages will not be as obvious.

If people live to be 100 years old, dogs live to be 20 years old. While this might seem like a good rule of thumb, it is very inaccurate. When trying to compare dog years to human years, you cannot make a generalization about all dogs. While some large-breed dogs do not last until ten years of age, the German Shepherd commonly lives to be 13 years of age, or more. Dogs generally are considered physically mature at three years of age (or earlier), but can

GETTING OLD
The bottom line is simply that your dog is getting old when you think he is getting old because he slows down in his level of general activity, including walking, running, eating, jumping and retrieving. On the other hand, the frequency of certain activities increases, such as more sleeping, more barking and more repetition of habits like going to the door without being called when you put your coat on to leave the house.

SENIOR SIGNS

An old dog starts to show one or more of the following symptoms:

• The hair on the face and paws starts to turn gray. The color breakdown usually starts around the eyes and mouth.

• Sleep patterns are deeper and longer, and the old dog is harder to awaken.

• Food intake diminishes.

• Responses to calls, whistles and other signals are ignored more and more.

• Eye contact does not evoke tail wagging (assuming it once did).

cases, until three years of age, though some dogs mature faster. Generally speaking, the first three years of a dog's life are like seven times that of comparable humans. That means a 3-year-old dog is like a 21-year-old human. As the curve of comparison shows, there is no hard and fast rule for comparing dog and human ages. Small breeds tend to live longer than large breeds, some breeds' adolescent periods last longer than others' and some breeds experience rapid periods of growth. The comparison is made even more difficult, for, likewise, not all humans age at the same rate...and human females live longer than human males.

reproduce even earlier. The German Shepherd is not considered physically mature, in some

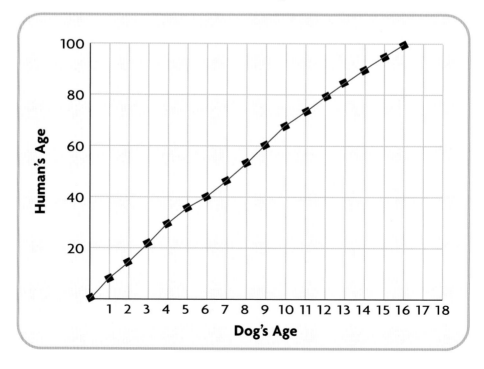

WHAT TO LOOK FOR IN SENIORS

Most vets and behaviorists use the seven-year-old mark as the time to consider a dog a "senior," though some breeders prefer to wait until the German Shepherd is eight or nine years of age. Nevertheless, the term "senior" does not imply that the dog is geriatric and has begun to fail in mind and body. Aging is essentially a slowing process. Humans readily admit that they feel a difference in their activity level from age 20 to 30, and then from 30 to 40, etc. By treating the seven-year-old dog as a senior, owners are able to implement certain therapeutic and preventative medical strategies with the help of their veterinarians. A senior-care program should include at least two veterinary visits per year and screening sessions to determine the dog's health status, as well as nutritional counseling. Vets determine the senior dog's health status through a blood smear for a complete blood count, serum chemistry profile with electrolytes, urinalysis, blood pressure check, electrocardiogram, ocular tonometry (pressure on the eyeball) and dental prophylaxis.

Such an extensive program for senior dogs is well advised before owners start to see the obvious physical signs of aging, such as slower and inhibited movement, graying, increased sleep/nap periods and disinterest in play and

NOTICING THE SYMPTOMS

The symptoms listed below are symptoms that gradually appear and become more noticeable. They are not life-threatening; however, the symptoms below are to be taken very seriously and warrant a discussion with your veterinarian:

- Your dog cries and whimpers when he moves, and he stops running completely.
- Convulsions start or become more serious and frequent. The usual convulsion (spasm) is when the dog stiffens and starts to tremble, being unable or unwilling to move. The seizure usually lasts for 5 to 30 minutes.
- Your dog drinks more water and urinates more frequently. Wetting and bowel accidents take place indoors without warning.
- Vomiting becomes more and more frequent.

other activity. This preventative program promises a longer, healthier life for the aging dog. Among the physical problems common in aging dogs are the loss of sight and hearing, arthritis, kidney and liver failure, diabetes mellitus, heart disease and Cushing's disease (a hormonal disease).

In addition to the physical manifestations discussed, there are some behavioral changes and problems related to aging dogs. Dogs suffering from hearing or vision loss, dental discomfort or arthritis can become aggressive. Likewise, the near-deaf and/or blind dog may be startled more easily and react in an unexpectedly aggressive manner. Seniors suffering from senility can become more impatient and irritable. Housesoiling accidents are associated with loss of mobility, kidney problems and loss of sphincter control as well as plaque accumulation, physiological brain changes and reactions to medications. Older dogs, just like young puppies, can suffer from separation anxiety, which can lead to excessive barking, whining, housesoiling and destructive behaviour. Seniors may become fearful of everyday sounds, such as vacuum cleaners, heaters, thunder and passing traffic. Some dogs have difficulty sleeping, due to discomfort, the need for frequent relief and the like.

Owners should avoid spoiling the older dog with too many fatty treats. Obesity is a common problem in older dogs and

If you are interested in locating a pet cemetery for your deceased dog, your vet may be of assistance.

subtracts years from their lives. Keep the senior dog as trim as possible, since excessive weight puts additional stress on the body's vital organs. Some breeders recommend supplementing the diet with foods high in fiber and lower in calories. Adding fresh vegetables and marrow broth to the senior's diet makes a tasty, low-calorie, low-fat supplement. Vets also offer specialty diets for senior dogs that are worth exploring.

Your dog, as he nears his twilight years, needs your patience and good care more than ever. Never punish an older dog for an accident or abnormal behavior. For all the years of love, protection and companionship that your dog has provided, he deserves special attention and courtesies. The older dog may need to relieve himself at 3 a.m. because he can no longer hold it for eight hours. Older dogs may not be able to remain crated for more than two or three hours. It may be time to give up a sofa or chair to your old friend. Although he may not seem as enthusiastic about your attention and petting, he does appreciate the considerations you offer as he gets older.

Your German Shepherd does not understand why his world is slowing down or growing quieter or dimmer. Owners must make their dogs' transition into their golden years as pleasant and rewarding as possible.

WHAT TO DO WHEN THE TIME COMES

You are never fully prepared to make a rational decision about putting your dog to sleep. It is very obvious that you love your German Shepherd or you would not be reading this book. Putting a beloved dog to sleep is extremely difficult. It is a decision that must be made with your vet. You are usually forced to make the decision when your dog experiences one or more life-threatening symptoms that have become serious enough for you to seek veterinary help.

If the prognosis of the malady indicates that the end is near and that your beloved pet will only continue to suffer and experience no enjoyment for the balance of his life, then euthanasia is the right choice.

WHAT IS EUTHANASIA?

Euthanasia derives from the Greek, meaning *good death*. In other words, it means the planned, painless killing of a dog suffering from a painful, incurable condition, or who is so aged that it cannot walk, see, eat or control its excretory functions. Euthanasia is usually accomplished by injection with an overdose of anesthesia or a barbiturate. Aside from the prick of the needle, the experience is usually painless.

MAKING THE DECISION

The decision to euthanize your dog is never easy. The days during which the dog becomes ill and the end occurs can be unusually stressful for you. If this is your first experience with the death of a loved one, you may need the comfort dictated by your religious beliefs. If you are the head of the family and have children, you should have involved them in the decision of putting your German Shepherd to sleep. Usually your dog can be maintained on drugs for a few days in order to give you ample time to make a decision. During this time, talking with members of your family or with people who have lived through the same experience can ease the burden of your inevitable decision.

THE FINAL RESTING PLACE

Dogs can have some of the same privileges as humans. The remains of your beloved dog can be buried in a pet cemetery, which is generally expensive. Dogs who have died at home can be buried on your property in a place suitably marked with some stone or newly planted tree or bush. Alternatively, your dog can be cremated individually and the ashes returned to you. A less expensive option is mass cremation, although, of course, the ashes cannot then be returned. Vets can usually arrange the cremation on your behalf. The cost of all of these options should always be discussed frankly and openly with your vet.

SHOWING YOUR
GERMAN SHEPHERD DOG

When you purchase your German Shepherd, you will make it clear to the breeder whether you want one just as a lovable companion and pet, or if you hope to be buying a German Shepherd with show prospects. No reputable breeder will sell you a young puppy and tell you that it is *definitely* of show quality, for so much can go wrong during the early months of a puppy's development. If you plan to show, what you will hopefully have acquired is a puppy with "show potential."

To the novice, exhibiting a German Shepherd in the show ring may look easy, but it takes an excellent dog, a lot of hard work and devotion to do top winning at a show such as the prestigious Westminster Kennel Club dog show, not to mention a little luck too!

AKC GROUPS

For showing purposes, the American Kennel Club divides its recognized breeds into seven groups: Sporting Dogs, Hounds, Working Dogs, Terriers, Toys, Non-Sporting Dogs and Herding Dogs (of which the German Shepherd is a member).

The first concept that the canine novice learns when watching a dog show is that each dog first competes against members of his own breed. Once the judge has selected the best member of each breed (Best of Breed), that chosen dog will compete with other Best of Breed dogs in his group. Finally, the dogs chosen first in each group will compete for Best in Show.

The second concept that you must understand is that the dogs are not actually compared against one another. The judge compares each dog against the breed standard, the written description of the ideal specimen that is approved by the American Kennel Club (AKC). While some early breed standards were indeed based on specific dogs that were famous or popular, many dedicated enthusiasts say that a perfect specimen, as described in the standard, has never walked into a show ring, has never been bred and, to the woe of dog breeders around the globe, does not exist. Breeders attempt to get as close to this ideal as possible with every litter, but theoretically the "perfect" dog is so elusive that it is impossible. (And if the

Opposite page: To pursue your dream of winning in the show ring, you will need to purchase a puppy from a proven line of champion dogs.

Dog shows are often held outdoors. These dogs are being run in front of the judges so their gaits can be evaluated.

"perfect" dog were born, breeders and judges would never agree that it was indeed "perfect.")

If you are interested in exploring the world of dog showing, your best bet is to join your local breed club or the national parent club, which is the German Shepherd Dog Club of America. These clubs often host both regional and national specialties, shows only for German Shepherds, which can include conformation as well as obedience, agility and herding trials. Even if you have no intention of competing with your German Shepherd, a specialty is like a festival for lovers of the breed who congregate to share their favorite topic: German Shepherds! Clubs also send out newsletters, and some organize training days and seminars in order that people may learn more about their chosen breed. To locate the breed club closest to you, contact the American Kennel Club, which furnishes the rules and regulations for all of these events plus general dog registration and other basic requirements of dog ownership.

In the US, the American Kennel Club offers three kinds of conformation shows: an all-breed show (for all AKC-recognized breeds), a specialty show (for one breed only, usually sponsored by the parent club) and a Group show (for all breeds in the Group).

For a dog to become an AKC champion of record, the dog must accumulate 15 points at the shows from at least three different judges, including two "majors." A "major" is defined as a three-, four- or five-point win, and the number of points per win is determined on the number of dogs entered in the show on the day. Depending on the breed, the number of points that are awarded varies. In a breed as popular as the German Shepherd, more dogs are needed to rack up the points. At any dog show, only one dog and one bitch of each breed can win points.

Dog showing does not offer "co-ed" classes. Dogs and bitches never compete against each other in the classes. Non-champion dogs are called "class dogs" because they compete in one of the five classes. Dogs are entered in a particular class depending on his age and previous show wins. To begin, there is the Puppy Class (for 6- to 9-month-olds and for 9- to 12-month-olds); this class is followed by the Novice Class (for dogs that have not won any first prizes except in the Puppy Class or three first prizes in the Novice Class and have not accumulated any points toward their champion title); the Bred-by-Exhibitor Class (for dogs handled by their breeders or handled by one of the breeder's immediate family); the American-bred Class (for dogs bred in the USA); and the Open Class (for any dog that is not a champion).

The judge at the show begins judging the Puppy Class, first dogs and then bitches, and proceeds through the classes. The judge places his winners first through fourth in each class. In the Winners Class, the first-place winners of each class compete with one another to determine Winners Dog and Winners Bitch. The judge also places a Reserve Winners Dog and Reserve Winners Bitch, which could be awarded the points in the case of a disqualification. The Winners Dog and Winners Bitch are the two that are awarded the points for the breed, then compete with any champions of record entered in the show. The judge reviews the Winners Dog, Winners Bitch and all the other champions to select his Best of Breed. The Best of Winners is selected between the Winners Dog and Winners Bitch. Were one of these two to be selected Best of Breed, it would automatically be named Best of Winners as well. Finally the judge selects his Best of Opposite Sex to the Best of Breed winner.

BECOMING A CHAMPION

An official AKC champion of record requires that a dog accumulate 15 points under three different judges, including two "majors" under different judges. Points are awarded based on the number of dogs entered into competition, varying from breed to breed and place to place. A win of three, four or five points is considered a "major." The AKC annually assigns a schedule of points to adjust to the variations that accompany a breed's popularity and the population of a given area.

At a Group show or all-breed show, the Best of Breed winners from each breed then compete against one another in their respective groups for Group One through Group Four. The judge compares each Best of Breed to his breed standard, and the dog that most closely lives up to the ideal for his breed is selected as Group One.

SHOW-RING ETIQUETTE

Just as with anything else, there is a certain etiquette to the show ring that can only be learned through experience. Showing your dog can be quite intimidating to you as a novice when it seems as if everyone else knows what he is doing. You can familiarize yourself with ring procedure beforehand by taking handling classes to prepare you and your dog for conformation showing and by talking with experienced handlers. When you are in the ring, it is very important to pay attention and listen to the instructions you are given by the judge about where to move your dog. Remember, even the most skilled handlers had to start somewhere. Keep it up and you too will become a proficient handler as you gain practice and experience.

Finally, all seven Group winners (from the Herding Group, Toy Group, Hound Group, etc.) compete for Best in Show.

To find out about dog shows in your area, you can subscribe to the American Kennel Club's monthly magazine, the *American Kennel Gazette,* and the accompanying *Events Calendar.* You can also look in your local newspaper for advertisements for dog shows in your area or go on the Internet to the AKC's website, http:www.akc.org.

If your German Shepherd is six months of age or older and registered with the AKC, you can enter him in a dog show where the breed is offered classes. Provided that your German Shepherd does not have a disqualifying fault, he can compete. Only unaltered dogs can be entered in a dog show, so if you have spayed or neutered your German Shepherd, you cannot compete in conformation shows. The reason for this is simple. Dog shows are the main forum to prove which representatives in a breed are worthy of being bred. Only dogs that have achieved championships—the AKC "seal of approval" for quality in pure-bred dogs—-should be bred. Altered dogs, however, can participate in other AKC events such as obedience trials and the Canine Good Citizen program.

HANDLING

Before you actually step into the ring, you would be well advised to sit back and observe the judge's ring procedure. If it is your first time in the ring, do not be over-anxious and run to the front of the line. It is much better to stand back and study how the exhibitor in front of you is performing. The judge asks each handler to "stack" the dog, hopefully showing the dog off to his best advantage. The judge will observe the dog from a distance and from different angles, and approach the dog to check his teeth, overall structure, alertness and muscle tone, as well as consider how well the dog "conforms" to the standard. Most importantly, the judge will have the exhibitor move the dog around the ring in some pattern that he should specify. Finally, the judge will give the dog one last look before moving on to the next exhibitor.

If you are not in the top four in your class at your first show, do not be discouraged. Be patient and consistent, and you may eventually

OBEDIENCE VICTOR/VICTRIX

In 1968, the German Shepherd Dog Club of America inaugurated a special award for the breed member who gained the highest combined obedience score for the year. Depending on the gender of the winner, the title of Obedience Victor or Obedience Victrix is bestowed upon the dog. The first Obedience Victrix was Heide von Zook, UDT (1968) and the first Obedience Victor was Schillenkamp Duke of Orleans, UDT (1970).

find yourself in a winning line-up. Remember that the winners were once in your shoes and have devoted many hours and much money to earn the placement. If you find that your dog is losing

Showing dogs can be big-time entertainment with expert handlers and beautiful dogs putting on quite a spectacle.

every time and never getting a nod, it may be time to consider a different dog sport or to just enjoy your German Shepherd as a pet. Parent clubs offer other events, such as agility, tracking, obedience, herding, instinct tests and more, which may be of interest to the owner of a well-trained German Shepherd.

OBEDIENCE TRIALS

Obedience trials in the US trace back to the early 1930s when organized obedience training was developed to demonstrate how well dog and owner could work together. The pioneer of obedience trials is Mrs. Helen Whitehouse Walker, a Standard Poodle fancier, who designed a series of exercises after the Associated Sheep, Police Army Dog Society of Great Britain. German Shepherd fancier Marie J. Leary worked alongside Mrs. Walker and trained many Shepherds to excel in this sport. Since the early days, obedience trials have grown by leaps and bounds, and today there are over 2,000 trials held in the US every year, with more than 100,000 dogs competing. Any registered AKC dog can enter an obedience trial, regardless of conformational disqualifications or neutering.

Obedience trials are divided into three levels of progressive difficulty. At the first level, the Novice, dogs compete for the title Companion Dog (CD); at the intermediate level, the Open, dogs compete for the title Companion Dog Excellent (CDX); and at the advanced level, dogs compete for the title Utility Dog (UD). A German Shepherd by the name of Ch. Schwarpels von Mardex, owned by W. P. Pheiffer, was the first to win all three titles. Miss Leary's Ch. Anthony of Cosalta distinguished himself as the first CDX winner. Classes are subdivided into "A" (for beginners) and "B" (for more experienced handlers). A perfect score at any level is 200, and a dog must score 170 or better to earn a "leg," of which three are needed to earn the title. To earn points, the dog must score more than 50% of the available points in each exercise; the possible points range from 20 to 40.

Each level consists of a different set of exercises. In the Novice level, the dog must heel on- and off-leash, come, long sit, long

NEATNESS COUNTS
Surely you've spent hours grooming your dog to perfection for the show ring, but don't forget about yourself! While the dog should be the center of attention, it is important that you also appear neat and clean. Wear smart, appropriate clothes and comfortable shoes in a color that contrasts with your dog's coat. Look and act like a professional.

Structure is tantamount to soundness in the German Shepherd Dog. Soundness is assessed by the judge by observing the dog's gait as he is moved around the ring.

down and stand for examination. These skills are the basic ones required for a well-behaved "Companion Dog." The Open level requires that the dog perform the same exercises but without a leash for extended lengths of time, as well as retrieve a dumbbell, broad jump and drop on recall. In the Utility level, dogs must perform ten difficult exercises, including scent discrimination, hand signals for basic commands, directed jump and directed retrieve.

Once a dog has earned the UD title, he can compete with other proven obedience dogs for the coveted title of Utility Dog Excellent (UDX), which requires that the dog win "legs" in ten shows.

Utility Dogs who earn "legs" in Open B and Utility B earn points toward their Obedience Trial Champion title. In 1977, the title Obedience Trial Champion (OTCh.) was established by the AKC. To become an OTCh., a dog needs to earn 100 points, which requires three first places in Open B and Utility under three different judges.

The Grand Prix of obedience trials, the AKC National Obedience Invitational gives qualifying Utility Dogs the chance to win the newest and highest title: National Obedience Champion (NOC). Only the top 25 ranked obedience dogs, plus any dog ranked in the top 3 in his breed, are allowed to compete.

AGILITY TRIALS

Having had its origins in the UK back in 1977, AKC agility had its official beginning in the US in August 1994, when the first licensed agility trials were held. The AKC allows all registered breeds (including Miscellaneous Class breeds) to participate, providing the dog is 12 months of age or older. Agility is designed so that the handler demonstrates how well the dog can work at his side. The handler directs his dog over an obstacle course that includes jumps as well as tires, the dog walk, weave poles, pipe tunnels, collapsed tunnels, etc. While working his way through the course, the dog must keep one eye and ear on the handler and the rest of his body on the course. The handler gives verbal and hand signals to guide the dog through the course.

The first organization to promote agility trials in the US was the United States Dog Agility Association, Inc. (USDAA), which was established in 1986 and spawned numerous member clubs around the country. Both the USDAA and the AKC offer titles to winning dogs. Three titles are available through the USDAA: Agility Dog (AD), Advanced Agility Dog (AAD) and Master Agility Dog (MAD). The AKC offers Novice Agility (NA), Open Agility (OA), Agility Excellent (AX) and Master Agility Excellent (MX). Beyond these four AKC titles, dogs can win additional ones in "jumper" classes, Jumpers with Weave Novice (NAJ), Open (OAJ) and Excellent (MXJ), which lead to the ultimate title(s): MACH, Master

Given the breed's natural desire to please and follow instructions, agility trials are an excellent forum for the Shepherd's talents. This talented dog is sailing through the weave poles.

Agility Champion. Dogs can continue to add number designations to the MACH titles, indicating how many times the dog has met the MACH requirements, such as MACH1, MACH2, etc.

Agility is great fun for dog and owner with many rewards for everyone involved. Interested owners should join a training club that has obstacles and experienced agility handlers who can introduce you and your dog to the "ropes" (and tires, tunnels, etc.).

TRACKING

Any dog is capable of tracking, using his nose to follow a trail. Tracking tests are exciting and competitive ways to test your German Shepherd's ability to search and rescue. The AKC started tracking tests in 1937, when the first AKC-licensed test took place as part of the Utility level at an obedience trial. Ten years later in 1947, the AKC offered the first title, Tracking Dog (TD). Noted obedience Shepherd, Ch. Schwarpels von Mardex, was the first German Shepherd to earn the TD title. It was not until 1980 that the AKC added the Tracking Dog Excellent (TDX) title, which was followed by the Versatile Surface Tracking (VST) title in 1995. The title Champion Tracker (CT) is awarded to a dog who has earned all three titles.

In the beginning level of tracking, the owner follows the dog through a field on a long leash. To earn the TD title, the dog must follow a track laid by a human 30 to 120 minutes prior. The track is about 500 yards with up to five directional changes. The TDX requires that the dog follow a track that is three to five hours old over a course up to 1,000 yards with up to seven directional changes. The VST requires that the dog follow a track up to five hours old through an urban setting.

HERDING TESTS AND TRIALS

Since the first sheepdog trials recorded in the late 19th century in Wales, the practice of herding trials

---

FIVE CLASSES AT SHOWS

At most AKC all-breed shows, there are five regular classes offered: Puppy, Novice, Bred by Exhibitor, American-bred and Open. The Puppy Class is usually divided as 6 to 9 months of age and 9 to 12 months of age. When deciding in which class to enter your dog, male or female, you must carefully check the show schedule to make sure that you have selected the right class. Depending on the age of the dog, its previous first-place wins and the sex of the dog, you must make the best choice. It is possible to enter a one-year-old dog who has not won sufficient first places in any of the non-Puppy Classes, though the competition is more intense the further you progress from the Puppy Class.

A well-trained German Shepherd has learned how to stand politely in the ring while the judge examines him.

has grown tremendously around the world. The first trial began as a friendly match to see which farmer's dog was the best at moving sheep. Today the sport is more organized than in those early days, and all Herding breeds can earn titles at these fun and competitive events.

The AKC offers herding trials and tests to any Herding dog that is nine months of age or older. The handler is expected to direct the German Shepherd to herd various livestock, including sheep, ducks, goats and cattle. There are two titles for herding tests, Herding Tested (HT) and Pre-Trial Tested (PT). If the dog shows a basic innate ability, he is awarded a HT title; the PT title is awarded to a dog that can herd a small herd of livestock through a basic course.

In herding trials, there are four titles awarded: Herding Started

(HS), Herding Intermediate (HI), Herding Excellent (HX) and Herding Champion (HCh.), the latter of which is awarded to a dog who has demonstrated mastery of herding in the most demanding of circumstances. Like shows, herding trials are judged against a set of standards as well as other dogs.

A distinct advantage to a large outdoor show is the size of the ring, allowing the handler to gait his dog without constraints.

To best understand the way the German Shepherd behaves, an owner must learn to "think like a dog."

BEHAVIOR OF YOUR
GERMAN SHEPHERD DOG

As a German Shepherd owner, you have selected your dog so that you and your loved ones can have a companion, a protector, a friend and a four-legged family member. You invest time, money and effort to care for and train the family's new charge. Of course, this chosen canine behaves perfectly! Well, perfectly *like a dog.*

THINK LIKE A DOG

Dogs do not think like humans, nor do humans think like dogs, though we try. Unfortunately, a dog is incapable of figuring out how humans think, so the responsibility falls on the owner to adopt a viable canine mindset. Dogs cannot rationalize, and dogs exist *in the present moment.* Many a

German Shepherds respond best to positive reinforcement and unmitigated praise.

dog owner makes the mistake in training of thinking that he can reprimand his dog for something the dog did a while ago. Basically, you cannot even reprimand a dog for something he did 20 seconds ago! Either catch him in the act or forget it! It is a waste of your and your dog's time—in his mind, you are reprimanding him for whatever he is doing at that moment.

The following behavioral problems represent some which owners most commonly encounter. Every dog is unique and every situation is unique. No author could purport for you to solve your German Shepherd's problem simply by reading a chapter in a breed book. So here we outline some basic "dogspeak" so that owners' chances of solving behavioral problems are increased. Discuss bad habits with your veterinarian and he can recommend a behavioral specialist to consult in appropriate cases. Since behavioral abnormalities are the leading reason for owners' abandoning their pets, we hope that you will make a valiant effort to solve your German Shepherd's problem. Patience and understanding are virtues that must dwell in every pet-loving household.

AGGRESSION

Aggression can be a very big problem in dogs. Aggression, when not controlled, becomes dangerous. An aggressive dog, no matter the size, may lunge at, bite or even attack a person or another dog. Aggressive behavior is not to be tolerated. It is more than just inappropriate behavior; it is not safe, especially with a large, powerful breed such as the

German Shepherd. It is painful for a family to watch their dog become unpredictable in his behavior to the point where they are afraid of the dog. And while not all aggressive behavior is dangerous, it can be frightening: growling, baring teeth, etc. It is important to get to the root of the problem to ascertain why the dog is acting in this manner. Aggression is a display of dominance, and the dog should not have the dominant role in his pack, which is, in this case, your family.

It is important not to challenge an aggressive dog as this could provoke an attack. Observe your German Shepherd's body language. Does he make direct eye contact and stare? Does he try to make himself as large as possible: ears pricked, chest out, tail erect? Height and size signify authority in a dog pack—being taller or "above" another dog literally means that he is "above" in the social status. These body signals tell you that your German Shepherd thinks he is in charge, a problem that needs to be dealt with. An aggressive dog is unpredictable in that you never know when he is going to strike and what he is going to do. You cannot understand why a dog that is playful and loving one minute is growling and snapping the next.

Fear is a common cause of aggression in dogs. If you can isolate what elicits the fear

The breed is prized for its calm demeanor and steady temperament. Only unscrupulous breeding or inappropriate training can ruin this "dog among dogs."

reaction, you can help the dog get over it. Supervise your German Shepherd's interactions with people and other dogs, and praise the dog when it goes well. If he starts to act aggressively in a situation, correct him and remove him from the situation. Do not let people approach the dog and start petting him without your express permission. That way, you can have the dog sit to accept petting, and praise him when he behaves acceptably. You are focusing on praise and on modifying his behavior by rewarding him when he acts appropriately. By being gentle and by supervising his interactions, you are showing him that there is no need to be afraid or defensive.

Dog fights can be instigated by a nervous owner pulling on the dog's leash, causing the dog to become agitated and act out.

If your dog exhibits aggressive tendencies, the best solution is to consult a behavioral specialist, one who has experience with the German Shepherd if possible. Together, perhaps you can pinpoint the cause of your dog's aggression and do something about it. An aggressive dog cannot be trusted, and a dog that cannot be trusted is not safe to have as a family pet. If the pet German Shepherd becomes untrustworthy, he cannot be kept in the home with the family. The family must get rid of the dog. In the very worst case, the dog must be euthanized.

AGGRESSION TOWARD OTHER DOGS
A dog's aggressive behavior toward another dog most likely stems from insufficient exposure to other dogs at an early age. If other dogs make your German Shepherd nervous and agitated, he will lash out as a protective mechanism. A dog who has not received sufficient exposure to

other canines tends to believe that he is the only dog on the planet. The animal becomes so dominant that he does not even show signs that he is fearful or threatened. Without growling or any other physical signal as a warning, he will lunge at and bite the other dog. A way to correct this is to let your German Shepherd approach another dog when walking on lead. Watch *very closely* and at the *very first* sign of aggression, correct your German Shepherd and pull him away. Scold him for any sign of discomfort, and then praise him when he ignores or tolerates the other dog. Keep this up until either he stops the aggressive behavior, learns to ignore the other dog or even accepts other dogs. Praise him lavishly for his correct behavior.

DOMINANT AGGRESSION
A social hierarchy is firmly established in a wild dog pack. The dog wants to dominate those under him and please those above him. Dogs know that there *must* be a leader. If you are not the obvious choice for emperor, the dog will assume the throne! These conflicting innate desires are what a dog owner is up against when he sets about training a dog. In training a dog to obey commands, the owner is reinforcing that he is the top dog in the pack and that the dog should, and should want

to, serve his superior. Thus, the owner is suppressing the dog's urge to dominate by modifying his behavior and making him obedient.

An important part of training is taking every opportunity to reinforce that you are the leader. The simple action of making your German Shepherd sit to wait for his food instead of allowing him to run up to get it when he wants it says that you control when he eats; he is dependent on you for food. Although it may be difficult, do not give in to your dog's wishes every time he whines at you or looks at you with pleading eyes. It is a constant effort to show the dog that his place in the pack is *at the bottom.* This is not meant to sound cruel or in-humane. You love your German

DOGGIE DEMOCRACY
Your dog inherited the pack-leader mentality. He only knows about pecking order. He instinctively wants to be "top dog," but you have to convince him that you are boss. There is no such thing as living in a democracy with your dog. You are the one who makes the rules.

FEAR FACTOR
Fear in a grown dog is often the result of improper or incomplete socializa-tion as a pup, or it can be the result of a traumatic experience he suffered when young. Keep in mind that the term "traumatic" is relative—something that you would not think twice about can leave a lasting negative impression on a puppy. If the dog experiences a similar experience later in life, he may try to fight back to protect himself. Again, this behavior is very unpredictable, especially if you do not know what is triggering his fear.

Shepherd and you should treat him with care and affection. You (hopefully) did not get a dog just so you could control another creature. Dog training is not about being cruel or feeling important, it is about molding the dog's behavior into what is acceptable and teaching him to live by your rules. In theory, it is quite simple: catch him in appropriate behavior and reward him for it. Add a dog into the equation and it becomes a bit more trying, but as a rule of thumb, positive reinforcement is what works best.

With a dominant dog, punish-ment and negative reinforcement can have the opposite effect of

THE MIGHTY MALE

Males, whether castrated or not, will mount almost anything: a pillow, your leg or, much to your dismay, even your neighbor's leg. As with other types of inappropriate behavior, the dog must be corrected while in the act, which for once is not difficult. Often he will not let go! While a puppy is experimenting with his very first urges, his owners feel he needs to "sow his oats" and allow the pup to mount. As the pup grows into a full-size dog, with full-size urges, it becomes a nuisance and an embarrassment. Males always appear as if they are trying to "save the race," more determined and stronger than imaginable. While altering the dog at an appropriate age will limit the dog's desire, it usually does not remove it entirely.

what you are after. It can make a dog fearful and/or act out aggressively if he feels he is being challenged. Remember, a dominant dog perceives himself at the top of the social heap and will fight to defend his perceived status. The best way to prevent that is to never give him reason to think that he is in control in the first place. If you are having trouble training your German Shepherd and it seems as if he is constantly challenging your authority, seek the help of an obedience trainer or behavioral specialist. A professional will work with both you and your dog to teach you effective techniques to use at home. Beware of trainers who rely on excessively harsh methods; scolding is necessary now and then, but the focus in your training should *always* be on positive reinforcement.

SEXUAL BEHAVIOR

Dogs exhibit certain sexual behaviors that may have influenced your choice of male or female when you first purchased your German Shepherd. Spaying/neutering will eliminate some of these behaviors, but if you are purchasing a dog that you wish to show or breed, you should be aware of what you will have to deal with throughout the dog's life.

Female dogs usually have two estruses per year, each season lasting about three weeks.

SMILE!

Dogs and humans may be the only animals that smile. A dog will imitate the smile on his owner's face when he greets a friend. The dog only smiles at his human friends; he never smiles at another dog or cat. Usually, a dog rolls up his lips and shows his teeth in a clenched mouth while rolling over onto his back, begging for a soft scratch.

These are the only times during which a female dog will mate, and she usually will not allow this until the second week of the cycle. If a bitch is not bred during the heat cycle, it is not uncommon for her to experience a false pregnancy, in which her mammary glands swell and she exhibits maternal tendencies toward toys or other objects.

Male dogs tend to wander away from home more, can be more dog-aggressive and can develop annoying marking and mounting behaviors. Undeniably obsessed with their scatalogical needs, males are more difficult to housebreak than females.

Owners must further recognize that mounting is not merely a sexual expression but also one of dominance, seen in dogs and bitches alike. Be consistent and persistent in discouraging this and you will find that you can "move mounters."

CHEWING

The national canine pastime is chewing! Every dog loves to sink his "canines" into a tasty bone or any other hard object. Dogs need to chew, to massage their gums, to make their new teeth feel better and to exercise their jaws. This is a natural behavior deeply imbedded in "all things canine." Our role as owners is not to stop chewing, but to redirect it to positive, chew-worthy objects. Be an informed owner and purchase proper chew toys for your German Shepherd, like strong nylon bones made for large dogs. Be sure that

Dogs love to chew and they can be trained to retrieve if their favorite chew toy is used as the token to be fetched.

Do not allow your German Shepherd to jump up when he greets you. Place him on all fours and then greet him calmly.

the devices are safe and durable, since your dog's safety is at risk. Again, the owner is responsible for ensuring a dog-proof environment. The best answer is prevention: that is, put your shoes, handbags and other tasty objects in their proper places (out of the reach of the growing canine mouth). Direct puppies to their toys whenever you see them tasting the furniture legs or your pant leg. Make a loud noise to attract the pup's attention and immediately escort him to his chew toy and engage him with the toy for at least four minutes, praising and encouraging him all the while.

Some trainers recommend deterrents, such as hot pepper or another bitter spice or a product designed for this purpose, to discourage the dog from chewing on unwanted objects. This is sometimes reliable, though not as often as the manufacturers of such products claim. Test out the product with your own dog before investing in large quantities.

JUMPING UP

Jumping up is a dog's friendly way of saying hello! Some dog owners do not mind when their dog jumps up, which is fine for them. The problem arises when guests come to the house and the dog greets them in the same manner— whether they like it or not! However friendly the greeting may be, chances are your visitors will not appreciate nearly being knocked over by 80 pounds of German Shepherd. The dog will not be able to distinguish upon whom he can jump and whom he cannot. Therefore, it is probably best to discourage this behavior entirely.

Pick a command such as "Off" (avoid using "Down" since you will use that for the dog to lie down) and tell him "Off" when he jumps up. Place him on the ground on all fours and have him sit, praising him the whole time. Always lavish him with praise and petting when he is in the sit position. That way you are still giving him a warm affectionate greeting, because you are as excited to see him as he is to see you!

DIGGING

Digging, which is seen as a destructive behavior to humans, is actually quite a natural behavior in dogs. Although the "earth dogs" (also known as terriers) are most closely associated with digging, any dog's desire to dig can be irrepressible and most frustrating to his owners. When digging occurs in your yard, it is actually a normal behavior redirected into something the dog can do in his everyday life. For example, in the wild, a dog would be actively seeking food, making his own shelter, etc. He would be using his paws in a purposeful manner; he would be using them for his survival. Since you provide him with food and shelter, he has no need to use his paws for these purposes, and so the energy that he would be using manifests itself in the form of little holes all over your garden and flower beds.

Perhaps your dog is digging as a reaction to boredom—it is somewhat similar to someone eating a whole bag of chips in front of the TV—because they are there and there is not anything better to do! Basically, the answer is to provide the dog with adequate play and exercise so that his mind and paws are occupied, and so that he feels as if he is doing something useful.

Of course, digging is easiest to control if it is stopped as soon as possible, but it is often hard to catch a dog in the act, especially if he is alone in the yard during the day. If your dog is a compulsive digger and is not easily distracted by other activities, you can designate an area on your property where it is okay for him to dig. If you catch him digging in an off-limits area of the yard, immediately bring him to the approved area and praise him for digging there. Keep a close eye on him so that you can catch him, that is the only way he is going to understand what is permitted and what is not. If you bring him to a hole he dug an hour ago and tell him "No," he will understand that you are not fond of holes, or dirt or flowers. If you catch him while he is stifle-deep in your tulips, that is when he will get your message.

BARKING

Dogs cannot talk—oh, what they would say if they could! Instead, barking is a dog's way of "talking." It can be somewhat

---

NO KISSES

We all love our dogs and our dogs love us. They show their love and affection by licking us. This is not a very sanitary practice, as dogs lick and sniff in some unsavory places. Kissing your dog on the mouth is strictly forbidden, as parasites can be transmitted in this manner.

Jumping and climbing come naturally to a dog as athletic as the German Shepherd. Be certain your property is securely fenced or your dog may venture off on his own.

frustrating because it is not always easy to tell what a dog means by his bark—is he excited, happy, frightened, angry? Whatever it is that the dog is trying to say, he should not be punished for barking. It is only when the barking becomes excessive, and when the excessive barking becomes a bad habit, does the behavior need to be modified.

If an intruder came into your home in the middle of the night and the dog barked a warning, wouldn't you be pleased? You would probably deem your dog a hero, a wonderful guardian and protector of the home. On the other hand, if a friend drops by unexpectedly and rings the doorbell and is greeted with a

sudden sharp bark, you would probably be annoyed at the dog. But isn't it just the same behavior? The dog does not know any better...unless he sees who is at the door and it is someone he is familiar with, he will bark as a means of vocalizing that his (and your) territory is being threatened. While your friend is not posing a threat, it is all the same to the dog. Barking is his means of letting you know that there is an intrusion, whether friend or foe, on your property. This type of barking is instinctive and should not be discouraged.

Excessive habitual barking, however, is a problem that should be corrected early on. As your German Shepherd grows up, you will be able to tell when his barking is purposeful and when it is for no reason. You will become able to distinguish your dog's different barks and with what they are associated. For example, the bark when someone comes to the door will be different from the bark when he is excited to see you. It is similar to a person's tone of voice, except that the dog has to rely totally on tone of voice because he does not have the benefit of using words. An incessant barker will be evident at an early age.

There are some things that encourage a dog to bark. For example, if your dog barks non-stop for a few minutes and you

A German Shepherd who gets regular exercise and play will be less likely to resort to destructive behavior.

give him a treat to quiet him, he believes that you are rewarding him for barking. He will associate barking with getting a treat, and

TRAINING TIP

To encourage proper barking, you can teach your dog the command "Quiet." When someone comes to the door and the dog barks a few times, praise him. Talk to him soothingly and, when he stops barking, tell him "Quiet" and continue to praise him. In this sense, you are letting him bark his warning, which is an instinctive behavior, and then rewarding him for being quiet after a few barks. You may initially reward him with a treat after he has been quiet for a few minutes.

will keep doing it until he is rewarded.

FOOD STEALING

Is your dog devising ways of stealing food from your counter tops? If so, you must answer the following questions: Is your German Shepherd hungry, or is he constantly famished like every other chow hound? Why is there food on the counter top? Face it, some dogs are more food-motivated than others; some dogs are totally obsessed by a slab of brisket and can only think of their next meal. Food stealing is terrific fun and always yields a great reward—*food*, glorious food.

The owner's goal, therefore, is to make the reward less rewarding,

This
German
Shepherd has a
most unique
approach to
begging.

This German Shepherd has a most unique approach to begging.

even startling! Plant a shaker can (an empty cola can with coins inside) on the counter so that it catches your pooch offguard. There are other devices available that will surprise the dog when he is looking for a mid-afternoon snack. Such remote-control devices, though not the first choice of some trainers, allow the correction to come from the object instead of the owner. These devices are also useful to keep the snacking hound from napping on furniture that is forbidden.

BEGGING

Just like food stealing, begging is a favorite pastime of hungry puppies! With that same reward—*food!* Dogs quickly learn that their owners keep the "good food" for themselves, and that we humans do not dine on kibble alone. Begging is a conditioned response related to a specific stimulus, time and place. The sounds of the kitchen, cans and bottles opening, crinkling bags, the smell of food

in preparation, etc., will excite the chow hound and soon the paws are in the air!

Here is the solution to stopping this behavior: Never give in to a beggar! You are rewarding the dog for sitting pretty, jumping up, whining and rubbing his nose into you by giving him that wonderful reward—food. By ignoring the dog, you will (eventually) force the behavior into extinction. Note that the behavior likely gets worse before it disappears, so be sure there are not any "softies" in the family who will give in to little "Oliver" every time he whimpers, "More, please."

SEPARATION ANXIETY

Your German Shepherd may howl, whine or otherwise vocalize his displeasure at your leaving the

---

SOUND BITES

When a dog bites, there is always a good reason for his doing so. Many dogs are trained to protect a person, an area or an object. When that person, area or object is violated, the dog will attack. A dog attacks with his mouth. He has no other means of attack.

If a dog is a biter for seemingly no reason, if he bites the hand that feeds him or if he snaps at members of your family, see your veterinarian or behaviorist immediately to learn how to modify the dog's behavior.

house and his being left alone. This is a normal behavior, but separation anxiety is more serious and can lead to destructive behavior. Your dog needs to learn that he will be fine on his own for a while and that he will not wither away if he is not attended to every minute of the day. In fact, constant attention can lead to separation anxiety in the first place. If you are endlessly coddling and cooing over your dog, he will come to expect this from you all of the time and it will be more traumatic for him when you are not there. Obviously, you enjoy spending time with your dog, and he thrives on your love and attention. However, it should not become a dependent relationship where he is heartbroken without you.

One thing you can do to minimize separation anxiety is to make your entrances and exits as low-key as possible. Do not give your dog a long drawn-out goodbye, and do not lavish him with hugs and kisses when you return. This is giving in to the attention that he craves, and it will only make him miss the lovefest more when you are away. Another thing you can try is to give your dog a treat when you leave; this will not only keep him occupied and keep his mind off the fact that you just left, but it will also help him associate your leaving with a pleasant experience.

An adult dog will often "play fight" with a pup to let the pup know his place in the pack. The pup's not being hurt—in fact, the adult knows exactly how to use his jaws gently in play.

You should accustom your puppy to being left alone incrementally. However, he should be secure in his crate rather than loose in the house or yard.

You may have to accustom your dog to being left alone in small increments, much like when you introduced your pup to his crate. Of course, when your dog starts whimpering as you approach the door, your first instinct will be to run to him and comfort him, but do not do it! Really—eventually he will adjust and be just fine if you take it in small steps. His anxiety stems from being placed in an unfamiliar situation; by familiarizing him with being alone, he will learn that he is okay. That is not to say you should purposely leave your dog home alone, but the dog needs to know that while he can depend on you for his care, you do not have to be by his side 24 hours a day.

When the dog is alone in the house, he should be confined to his crate or a designated dog-proof area of the house. This should be the area in which he sleeps, so he should already feel comfortable there and this should make him feel more at ease when he is alone. This is just one of the many examples in which a crate is an invaluable tool for you and your dog, and another reinforcement of why your dog should view his crate as a happy place, a place of his own.

COPROPHAGIA

Feces eating is, to most humans, one of the most disgusting

behaviors that our dogs could engage in, yet to dogs it is perfectly normal. It is hard for us to understand why a dog would want to eat its own feces; he could be seeking certain nutrients that are missing from his diet, he could be just plain hungry, or he could be attracted by the pleasing (to a dog) scent. While coprophagia most often refers to the dog eating his own feces, a dog may likely eat that of another animal as well if he comes across it. Dogs often find the stool of cats and horses more palatable than that of other dogs. Vets have found that diets with a low digestibility, containing relatively low levels of fiber and high levels of starch, increase coprophagia. Therefore, high-fiber diets may decrease the likelihood of dogs eating feces. Both the consistency of the stool (how firm it feels in the dog's mouth) and the presence of undigested nutrients increase the likelihood. Once the dog

develops diarrhea from feces eating, it will likely quit this distasteful habit.

To discourage this behavior, first make sure that the food you are feeding your dog is nutritionally complete and that he is getting enough food. If changes in his diet do not seem to work, and no medical cause can be found, you will have to modify the behavior through environmental control before it becomes a habit. There are some tricks you can try, such as adding an unpleasant-tasting substance to the feces to make them unpalatable or adding something to the dog's food that will make it unpleasant tasting after it passes through the dog. The best way to prevent your dog from eating his stool is to make it unavailable—clean up after he eliminates and remove any stool from the yard. If it is not there, he cannot eat it.

Never reprimand the dog for stool eating, as this rarely impresses the dog. Vets recommend distracting the dog while he is in the act of stool eating. Another option is to muzzle the dog when he is in the yard to relieve himself; this usually is effective within 30 to 60 days. Coprophagia most frequently is seen in pups 6 to 12 months of age, and usually disappears around the dog's first birthday.

NO BUTTS ABOUT IT!

Dogs get to know each other by sniffing each other's backsides. It seems that each dog has a telltale odor, probably created by the anal glands. It also distinguishes sex and signals when a female will be receptive to a male's attention. Some dogs snap at another dog's intrusion of their private parts.

INDEX

My German Shepherd

PUT YOUR PUPPY'S FIRST PICTURE HERE

Dog's Name _____

Date _____ Photographer _____